BIBLIOGRAPHIA

TRIPOTAMOPOLITANA

A Series of Bibliographies
published occasionally by
the Barbour Library
Pittsburgh Theological Seminary

General Editor: Dikran Y. Hadidian

Number VII

A ZWINGLI BIBLIOGRAPHY

The Clifford E. Barbour Library
Pittsburgh Theological Seminary
Pittsburgh, Pennsylvania

A ZWINGLI BIBLIOGRAPHY

Compiled by
H. Wayne Pipkin
Baylor University

The Clifford E. Barbour Library
Pittsburgh Theological Seminary
Pittsburgh, Pennsylvania

Clifford E. Barbour Library, Pittsburgh Theological Seminary

T A B L E   O F   C O N T E N T S

1

Preface

The purpose of this bibliography is to provide the
Reformation and Zwingli researcher with a comprehensive
listing of Zwingli literature and sources since 1897, the
year in which Georg Finsler's <u>Zwingli-Bibliographie</u> first
appeared. In addition, some pre-1897 articles and books
which were left out of the Finsler work have been included.
A further feature of this bibliography is the inclusion
of a wide selection of reviews and critical replies to
various books and articles.

The project was first announced in 1967. The initial
impetus for the collection came from Professor Ford Lewis
Battles, Professor of Church History at the Pittsburgh
Theological Seminary. Professor Battles is also respon-
sible for the bibliography's appearing in this series.
The compiler traveled extensively to many libraries, both
here and abroad in order to collect the present materials.
These journeys include three separate visits to the libraries of Zurich. Although the work is intended to be
comprehensive this writer is aware that gaps are unavoid-
able. The decision was made early to include as many reviews as possible. Even though no claims to completeness
can be advanced with regard to reviews, a wide sampling
has been obtained. This listing of reviews will assist

the scholar in obtaining a critical awareness of the issues involved in the Zwinglian Reformation.

The format of the bibliography is designed to facilitate its use. Part One is a listing, alphabetical by author, of the Zwingli literature. Part Two gives an alphabetical arrangement, usually by editor or translator, of the works of Zwingli. This latter part is divided into two sections: first, the collected writings or selections of Zwingli which appear in anthologies, and second, the individual writings of Zwingli. Two indices are included: an index of reviewers and an index of subjects.

The user of this bibliography should consult the body of the work if the name of the author is known; otherwise, the user should refer first to the subject index where he will find a list of the numbers appropriate for his consultation. The works of Zwingli are indexed according to the title of the original, unless there are translations listed. A list of abbreviations is added as a key to the periodicals abbreviated. Where the numeral precedes the date of the periodical the volume number is indicated. If available the issue number follows the volume number. Where no volume number is available the issue number follows the year or date of the periodical. The page or column numbers are given last where available. Occasionally the compiler failed to obtain a volume number, date, issue number or list of pages. Such omissions, even though rare, are regrettable. Hopefully, enough information is given to make it possible for the researcher to obtain the materials listed. It seemed the wiser course of action to include these few incomplete references as given rather than either to omit them or to prolong the publication of the bibliography in what would be essentially a fruitless line of investigation. Reviews and replies follow the entry reviewed and introduced by the letter R. Those works which are not normally of use for the historian--works of fiction, drama, poetry and music--are designated by the symbol [*] following the entry. Those works which this writer has deemed to be of particular value or significance are designated by the # sign preceding the entry number. Such a designation does not mean that other works are not of value, but that these designated entries are of more than average significance. These assessments of value are intended for the non-specialist or the researcher who makes only occasional forays into the territory of the German Swiss Reformation. Numbers 83, 257-77, 417, 1194 are not used. Since the numbering is arbitrary such an omission will not create difficulties for the user of the bibliog-raphy. Where possible the American custom of supplying the name of the publisher for books has been followed. Umlauts are used for words used in a German context. Otherwise, the English spelling is observed.

The compiler would like to express his gratitude to the library staffs at the following institutions or libraries: Case Memorial Library, Hartford Seminary Foundation; Andover-Harvard Library, Harvard Divinity School; Union Theological Seminary of New York; New York City Public Library; Library of Congress; Rice University; Moody Memorial Library, Baylor University; Southwestern Baptist Theological Seminary; Foundation for Reformation Research, St. Louis, Missouri; Staatsarchiv of Zurich, Switzerland; Zentralbibliothek, Zurich; Universitätsbibliothek, Vienna, Austria; Nationalbibliothek, Vienna; Staatsarchiv, Vienna. A Graduate Faculty Research Grant at Baylor University contributed to the project. Thanks are due to Elvin Johnson and Larry Braidfoot for their help in finding articles and reviews. Gratitude is extended to the following typists: Alice Ketchand, Sharon Hamil, Arlene Pipkin and Valerie Browning, who also prepared the Index of Reviewers. I would also like to thank the following: Professor Jochem Burckhardt, who helped unravel some obscure meanings; Professor Hans Hillerbrand for providing a lost reference; Professor Ralph Lynn for

5

supplying the quotation from Lewis Carrol; Professor Eberhard
von Waldow for reading the manuscript and for making numerous
suggestions; Sally Seidel for making the final corrections.
Professor Ford Lewis Battles has provided uncommon expertise
and encouragement during the course of this project. His
invaluable assistance has been gratefully received. Professor
G. R. Potter, formerly of Sheffield University, checked
the penultimate copy against his own files and the files
in Zurich and made untiring suggestions and improvements
on the bibliography. Professor Potter has been available
for consultation at every stage of the project and if there
is any value in this work, it is due in large part to him.
The world of Zwingli and Reformation research eagerly awaits
his biography of Zwingli which was nearing completion at
this writing.

In addition to the standardized abbreviations which
are deciphered on the Abbreviations page, shortened forms
of words are often used. Rather than create new abbreviations
the compiler relied on common usage, especially as found
in the bibliographies of Paul Sieber (No. 1228) and Willy
Wuhrmann (No. 1448) and the standard bibliography -- Karl
Schottenloher, Bibliographie zur deutschen Geschichte im
Zeitalter der Glaubensspaltung, 1517-1585, 6 vols. Leipzig,
1933-39. The compiler would also like to express his gratitude to
his wife, Arlene.

Abbreviations

Periodicals

AHR   American Historical Review
Archiv Archiv für Reformationsgeschichte
HZ   Historische Zeitschrift
JCH   Church History
JCS   Journal of Church and State
JEH   Journal of Ecclesiastical History
MQR   Mennonite Quarterly Review
NZZ   Neue Zürcher Zeitung
RHPR   Revue d'Histoire et de Philosophie Religieuses
SJT   Scottish Journal of Theology
SZG   Schweizerische Zeitschrift für Geschichte
ThL   Theologische Literaturzeitung
ThZ   Theologische Zeitschrift
ZKG   Zeitschrift für Kirchengeschichte
ZSKG   Zeitschrift für Schweizerische Kirchengeschichte
ZWA   Zwingliana

Other Abbreviations

Bez.   der Bezirk
N. F. Neue Folge
Recommended works
[*]   Drama, poetry, music, literature

To GEORGE and RAY POTTER,

"I never ask advice about growing," Alice said indignantly.
"Too proud?" Humpty Dumpty inquired.
Alice felt even more indignant at this suggestion.
"I mean," she said, "that one cannot help growing old."
"One can't, perhaps," said Humpty Dumpty, "but two can."

Lewis Carrol, _Alice Through the Looking Glass_

I. Zwingli Literature

1. Abelous, Louis. "Zwingli." Les pères de réformation. Paris, 1879. pp. 109 ff.

2. Aeppli, A. "Zwinglis Tod." Volkszeitung d. Bez. Pfäffikon, 1931. Nr. 122. [*]

3. Altherr, A. "Für unsere Kinder." Schweizerisches Protestantenblatt, 6, December 29, 1883, 426-430.

4. Altherr, W. "Zwingli und die Wiedertäufer." Evangelischer Kirchenbote für das Rheintal, 1918, pp. 2 ff.

5. Amacher, Ernst. "Zwingli als Volksmann." Kirchenbote für den Kanton Zürich, 1931. Nr. 10.

6. Andres, H. K. "Ulrich Zwingli - ein Dieb?" Heimatblüt, Gemeindeblatt der evangelisch-reformierten Kirchgemeinde Belp, 5, 1928. Nr. 2.

7. Appenzeller, Gotthold. "Die Beteiligung Solothurns am 2. Kappelerkrieg von 1531." Sonntagsblatt der Solothurner Zeitung, 1931, 15-28.

8. _____. "Was hat die schweizerische Landwirtschaft Ulrich Zwingli zu verdanken?" Solothurner Zeitung, 1931. Nr. 237.

9. Apple, Thomas G. "Zwingli and the Swiss Reformation." A Sermon preached in Harrisburg, Pa., January 6, 1884. Harrisburg, Pa.: The Telegraph Printing House, 1884.

10. Ardey, Cadonau. "La mort ded Ulrich Zwingli, ils 31 d'oct. 1531." Per Mintga Gi, 1931, 29-32.

11. Arx, Cäsar von. Brüder in Christo. Schriftenreihe des Schauspielhauses Zürich, X. Zurich: Oprecht, 1947. [*]
    R: Paul Kamer, Neue Zürcher Nachrichten, 1947. Nr. 50, 56.

12. Auer, Karl. "Bedarf es im gegenwärtigen Stadium der Theologie einer Zwingli-renaissance?" Volk und Kirche, 1931. Nr. 43.

9

13. Auer, Karl. "Zwingli-Gedächtnis." Volk und
    Kirche, 1931. Nr. 41.

14. Bader, R. "Die Reformation und ihr Einfluss auf
    das zürcherische Recht." Theologische Zeitschrift
    a. d. Schweiz, 19, 1902, 9-19.

15. Baer, Alfred. "Die Opfer der Kappeler Schlacht
    aus dem Pfarrstande." Kirchenbote für den
    Kanton Zürich, 1931. Nr. 9.

16. Bähler, Eduard. "Ein Gerücht über Zwinglis Tod aus
    dem Jahre 1569." ZWA, 4, 1, 1921, 26.

17. _____. "War Ursula Tremp die Schwester Zwinglis?"
    ZWA, 4, 1, 1921, 21-26.

18. Baiter, Hans. "Allerlei zu Ehren unseres Reformators
    Ulrich Zwingli." Relig. Volksblatt, 28, 1897, pp.
    212 ff. and 240 ff.

19. _____. "Ein Bild Zwinglis." NZZ, 1898. Nr. 118.

20. _____. "Die einstige Zwingli-Statue in Winterthur."
    ZWA, 2, 1, 1905, 5-6.

21. _____. "Gerold Meyer von Knonau, der Schüler und
    Freund Zwinglis." Kirchliches Jahrbuch der
    reformierten Schweiz, 4, 1898, pp. 29 ff.

22. _____. "Die Rückkehr der Waffen Zwinglis nach
    Zürich." ZWA, 1, 7, 1900, 133-137. Also: NZZ,
    1899. Nr. 302.

23. _____. "Ulrich Zwingli und Gerold Meyer von
    Knonau." ZWA, 1, 8, 1900, 161-163.

24. _____. "Zur Zwinglistatue von L. Keiser."
    ZWA, 2, 2, 1905, 64.

25. _____. "Zwinglihütte und Zwinglimuseum." Schweiz.
    Protestantenblatt, 20, 1897, pp. 142 ff.

26. _____. "Das Zwinglimuseum in Zürich." Schweiz.
    Protestantenblatt, 20, 1897, pp. 295 ff.

27. _____. "Zwinglistätten in Alt-Zürich." ZWA 1, 13,
    1903, 329-332.

28. Baiter, Hans. "Der Zwinglistein." Schweiz. Protestantenblatt, 22, 1899, pp. 61 ff.

29. Bakel, H. A. van. "Zwingli oder Luther?" ZFK, 52, 1933, 237-262. Also: Nieuw theolog. Tijdschrift, 21, 1932.
    R: W. Köhler, Theolog. Rundschau, 4, 1932.

30. Barth, Hans. "Eine Volksausgabe der Werke Zwinglis." NZZ, 1940. Nr. 1262.

31. Barth, Peter. "Ein Friedenstraktat Zwinglis." Die Christliche Welt, 1931. Nr. 19.

32. _____. "Zwingli: Zum 400 jährigen Gedächtnis seines Todestages." Zeitwende, 7, 1931, 344-356.

33. _____. "Zwinglis Beitrag zum Verständnis der biblischen Botschaft." Reformierte Kirchenzeitung, Wupperthal, 1931. Nr. 81.

34. Bäschlin, Conrad. "Geht uns Zwinglis Tod am 11. Okt. 1531 etwas an?" Mitteilungen a. d. Neuen Mädchen- schule, Bern, 70, 1931, 69-79.

35. _____. Zwingli und Wir. Bern: G. A. Bäschlin, 1919.

36. Basler, Hermann. "Zwingli und wir." Für Stadt und Land. Supplement of the N. Aargauer Zeitung, 1931. Nr. 4.

37. Bauer, Karl. "Die Abendmahlslehre Zwinglis bis zum Beginn der Auseinandersetzung mit Luther." Theologische Blätter, 5, 1926, 217-266.

38. _____. "Symbolik und Realpräsenz in der Abendmahls- anschauung Zwinglis bis 1525." ZFK, 46, 1928, 97-105.
    R: W. Köhler, HZ, 1928, 137.

39. Baumgartner, Albert. "Auf den Todestag Zwinglis." Emmentaler Tagbl., 1931. Nr. 476.

40. Baumgartner, Hans. "Zwinglis Frömmigkeit." Kirchenbote für den Kanton Zürich, 1931. Nr. 10.

41. Baumgartner, Otto. "Ulrich Zwingli." Encyclop. Handbuch d. Pädagogik. Edited by W. Rein. Vol. 7. Langensalza, 1899. pp. 909 ff.

42. Baur, August. "Zur Vorgeschichte der Disputation
     von Baden 1526." ZKG, 21, 1900, 91-111.

#43. _____. Zwinglis Theologie, ihr Werden und ihr
     System. 2 vols. Halle: Max Niemeyer, 1885, 1889.

44. Baur, Hans. "Einen andern Geist." Die freie
     Volkskirche, 1931. Nr. 21.

45. _____. "Das Labyrinth." Schweiz. Protestanten-
     blatt, 1919, pp. 2 ff.

46. _____. "Zwingli im Bilde." Schweiz. Protestanten-
     blatt, 1919, pp. 175 ff.

47. _____. "Zwingli, een wegwijzer uit de religieuse
     nooden van het heden." Ons godsdienstig Leven,
     Hoorn, 1931. Nr. 40.

48. _____. "Zwinglis Briefe." Schweiz. Protestanten-
     blatt, 1918, pp. 386 ff.

49. _____. Zwinglis Gattin Anna Reinhart; die erste
     Pfarrfrau der Schweiz. Zurich: Beer and Cie, 1918.
     R: G. Meyer von Knonau, ZWA, 3, 14, 1919, 472.

50. Baur, I. "Eine innere Begegnung mit Zwingli."
     Protestant, 34. Nr. 20.

51. Bender, M. E. "Zwingli and the Anabaptists in
     Caesar von Arx's drama 'Brueder in Christo'."
     MQR, 34, April 1960, 116-27.

#52. Bender, Wilhelm. Zwinglis Reformationsbündnisse.
     Zurich/Stuttgart: Zwingli Verlag, 1970.

53. Bendiscioli, M., and Colpo, M. "Zwingli, Huldrych
     (Ulrico Zuinglio)." Enciclopedia Filosofica.
     Vol. 4. Venezia-Roma: Instituto per la Collaborazione
     Culturale, 1957. 1842-43.

54. Berchtold-Belart, Jakob. "Zwingli im Spiegel von
     Zeitgenossen." Zürcher Post, 1931. Nr. 238.

55. _____. Das Zwinglibild und die ersten zürcherischen
     Reformationschroniken. Gräfenhainichen: C. Schulze
     and Co., 1928. [Zurich dissertation]

12

#56. Berchtold-Belart, Jakob. Das Zwinglibild und die
Zürcherischen Reformationschroniken. Eine text-
kritische Untersuchung. Quellen und Abhandlungen
zur schweizerischen Reformationsgeschichte, V.
Leipzig: M. Hensius Nachfolger Eger and Sievers,
1929.
    R: O.Farner, ZWA, 5, 3, 1930, 130-131; W. Köhler,
    NZZ, 1929. Nr. 1006; Theolog. Rundschau, N.F. 4,
    1932.

57. Bernold, Franz Joseph Benedikt. "Zwinglis Geist."
Aus den Papieren des Barden von Riva. Edited by
Ernst Götzinger. Mitteilungen zur vaterländischen
Geschichte, XXIV, 3. Folge. St. Gallen, 1891.
448-449.

58. _____. "Zwinglis Tod." Zürcher Taschenbuch auf
das Jahr 1907. Zurich, 1907. 109-110.

59. Bernoulli, August. "Eine zürcherische Verlustliste
von der Schlacht bei Kappel." Anzeiger für Schweiz.
Geschichte, 8, pp. 200 ff.

60. Bernoulli, Carl Albrecht. Ulrich Zwingli. Berlin:
S. Fischer, 1905. [*]

61. _____. "Zwingli in Wirklichkeit." NZZ, 1904.
Nrs. 343-344. [*]

62. Bernoulli, Edward. "Cosmas Alders Komposition auf
Zwingli's Tod." ZWA, 2, 5, 1907, 136-144. [*]

63. _____. "Zwei vierstimmige Sätze von Zwingli
Kappeler-Lied." ZWA, 3, 12/13, 1918/19, 404-413. [*]

64. Bertoliatti, Francesco. "Ulrico Zwingli e la guerra
di Musso, con una breve appendice su 'La dottrina
zwingliana nei Baliaggi e in Italia (1531-1532)'"
Svizzera Italiana Anno VII, 64. Luglio-Agosto,
1947. 298-309.

65. Bessler, Hans. "Der neue Zwinglibrunnen zu Wildhaus."
ZWA, 9, 10, 1953, 601-602.

66. Beurle, Elsa. Der politische Kampf um die religiöse
Einheit der Eidgenossenschaft 1520-1527: Ein
Beitrag zu Zwinglis Staatspolitik. Linz, 1920.

13

67. Bichon, J. "La doctrine de la Sante-Cène chez
     Luther, Zwingli et Calvin." Foi et Vie, 43, 4, 1946,
     404-409.

68. Biordi, Raffaello. "Zwingli a Clemente VII per una
     fattura insoluta." Almanacco de bibliotecari
     italiani, 1959, 173-180.

69. Bircher, Eugen. "Ulrich Zwinglis militärische
     Auffassungen." Allgemeine schweizerische
     Militärzeitung, 1931. Nr. 10.

70. Birnbaum, N. "The Zwinglian Reformation in Zürich."
     Archives de sociologie des religions, 4, 8, 1959,
     15-30.

71. _____. "The Zwinglian Reformation in Zürich."
     Past and Present, 1959, 15, 27-47.

72. Birnstiel, J. G. "Zwingli als Charakter." Schweiz.
     Verein für freies Christentum. II, 1907. Zurich: August
     Frick.

73. Blanke, Fritz. "Antwort auf Wilhelm Niesel: Zwinglis
     'spätere Sakramentanschauung'." Theologische
     Blätter, 1932, 1, col. 18.

74. _____. "Aus der Arbeit der kritischen Zwingli-
     Ausgabe." Schweizerische Theol. Umschau, 30, 3,
     October 1960, 146-150.

75. _____. Aus der Welt der Reformation. Fünf Aufsätze
     mit einer Liste der Veröffentlichungen des
     Verfassers. Zurich: Zwingli Verlag, 1960.
         R: Lothar Schreiner, South East Asia Journal of
     Theology, 3, 1961, 73-78; John H. Yoder, MQR,
     38, July 1964, 307-308; J. D. Burger, ThZ, 16,
     1960, 496-497; C. S. Meyer, Concordia Theological
     Monthly, 32, May 1961, 301; B. Moeller, HZ, 193,
     December 1961, 745.

76. _____. "Calvins Urteil über Zwingli." NZZ, 1936.
     Nr. 1022. Also: Aus der Welt der Reformation,
     18-47. Also: ZWA, 11, 2 , 1959, 66-92.

77. _____. "Fragen um ein Cranach-Bild." Theologische
     Zeitschrift, 1951, 467-471.

14

78. _____. "Gedanken zur Frage der Eigenart Zwinglis."
Der Kirchenfreund, 65, 20/21, 1931, 305-310, 322-
327.

79. _____. Huldrych Zwingli zum Gedächtnis seines
Todes am 11. Oktober 1531. Zurich, 1931.

80. _____. "Eine Kindheitserinnerung Zwinglis." NZZ,
1935. Nr. 1049.

81. _____. "'Luther an F. Pistorius in Nürnberg' and
'Votum Zwinglis an der Berner Disputation 1528'."
Katalog der Ausstellung "Genie und Handschrift."
Zurich: Artemisverlag, 1952. 60-61, 62-64.

82. _____. "Luther, Zwingli, Calvin." Der Gott der
Wahrheit. Edited by Eberhard Müller. Stuttgart:
Furcheverlag, 1936. 263-275. Also: Die Furche,
36, 1936, 421-431.

84. _____. "Miszelle zur Zwingliforschung: 'Der fry-
taglich predicant in Caesarea'." ThZ, 1951,
396-397.

85. _____. "Miszelle zur Zwingliforschung 'Der
heylige oder fromme Mann'." ThZ, 1951, 318-319.

86. _____. "Ein Neues Zwingli-Bildnis?" NZZ, 1951.
Nr. 1370.

87. _____. "Nochmals: Ein neues Zwingli-Bildnis?"
NZZ, 1951. Nr. 1672.

88. _____. "Petrus in Spänen." ThZ, 1952, 156.

89. _____. "Ulrich Zwingli." Sachwörterbuch der
Deutschkunde, 2, 1930, p. 1285 f.

90. _____. Ulrich Zwingli. Erlenbach Zurich: E. Reutsch,
1940.

91. _____. "Zu Zwinglis Entwicklung." Kirchenblatt
für die reformierte Schweiz, 86, 13, 1930, p. 197 f.

92. _____. "Zu Zwinglis Vorrede an Luther in der
Schrift 'Amica Exegesis', 1527." ZWA, 5, 4, 1930,
185-192.

93.   Blanke, F. "Zum Verständnis der Abendmahlslehre
       Zwinglis." Monatsschrift für Pastoraltheologie,
       27, 1931, 314-320.

94.   _____. "Zürcherische Theologenschulung von
       Zwingli bis heute." Kirchenbote für den Kanton
       Zürich, 46, 10, October 1960, 1-2.

95.   _____. "Zwingli." Die Furche, 25, 1939, 424-429.

96.   _____. "Zwingli, Leben und Schriften." Die
       Religion in Geschichte und Gegenwart. Vol. VI.
       Tübingen, 1963. 1952-1969.

97.   _____. "Zwingli mit Ambrosius Blarer im Gespräch."
       Der Konstanzer Reformator Ambrosius Blarer 1492-
       1564. Gedenkschrift zu seinem 400. Todestag.
       Konstanz/Stuttgart, 1964. 81-86. Also:
       Mennonitische Geschichtsblätter, 23, 1966, 24-29.

98.   _____. "Zwingli und Luther." NZZ, 1931. Nr. 1918.

99.   _____. "Zwingli, Eine Radiorede." Der Kirchen-
       freund, 68, 1934, 2-6.

100.   _____. "Zwingli und die zürcherische Reformation."
       NZZ, 1951. Nr. 419.

#101. _____. "Zwinglis Beitrag zur reformatorischen
       Botschaft." ZWA, 5, 5/6, 1931, 262-275.

102.   _____. "Zwinglis Fidei ratio, 1530; Entstehung
       und Bedeutung." Archiv, 57, 1/2, 1966, 96-102.

103.   _____. "Zwinglis Theologiestudium." Theologische
       Blätter, 1936, 3/4, 94-95.

104.   _____. "Zwinglis 'Prophezei' und die Anfänge des
       Puritanismus." NZZ, 1939. Nr. 1175.

105.   _____. "Zwinglis Sakramentanschauung."
       Theologische Blätter, 1931, 283-290.
       R: W. Köhler, Theolog. Rundschau, 4, 1932,
       col. 8 ff.

#106. _____. "Zwinglis Urteile über sich selbst." Die
       Furche, 22, 1936, 31-39. Also: Aus der Welt der
       Reformation, 9-17.

107. Blanke, F. "Das Zwinglistandbild in Kassel."
     ZWA, 7, 4, 1940, 272.

108. Boesch, Paul. "Die Beziehungen zwischen dem
     Toggenburg und Zürich seit der Reformation bis
     zum Ende des 17. Jahrhunderts." SZG, 12, 2, 1932.

     R: L. von Muralt, ZWA, 7, 5, 1941, 333.

109. _____. "Die Bildnisse von Huldrich Zwingli."
     Toggenburgerblätter für Heimatkunde, 13, 1950,
     1-16.

110. _____. "Homer im humanistischen Zürich." ZWA,
     8, 7, 1947, 390-398.

111. _____. "Wilhelm Zwingli in Strassburg (1539)."
     ZWA, 9, 1, 1949, 52-53.

112. _____. "Der Zürcher Apelles. Neues zu den
     Reformatorenbildnissen von Hans Asper." ZWA, 9,
     1, 1949, 16-43.

113. _____. "Zwingli-Gedichte (1539) des Andreas
     Zebedeus und des Rudolph Gwalther." ZWA, 9, 2,
     1950, 208-220.

114. Böhringer, Hans. "Zwingli und die Gerechtigkeit."
     Aufbau, 12. Nr. 42.

115. _____. "Zwinglis Testament für unser Geschlecht."
     St. Galler Stadtanzeiger, January 4, 1919. Nr. 3.

116. Boller, Max. "Gotteswort und Bibelwort."
     Protestant, 34. Nr. 20.

117. _____. "Was Zwingli an unserer heutigen Zürcher
     Kirche freuen wurde." Kirchenbote für den
     Kanton Zürich, 1931. Nr. 10.

118. Bolliger, Theodore P. Huldreich Zwingli; reformer
     and patriot, founder of the Reformed Churches,
     1484-1531. 1931.

119. _____. "Zwingli in Amerika." Reformierte
     Schweizerische Zeitung, 1932. Nr. 12.

120. Bolt, Niklaus. "Zwinglis Predigt und ihre Wirkung."
      Volkskalender für die reformierte Schweiz, 1940,
      38-43.

121. Bomberger, J. H. A. "Zwingli as a commentator."
      Mercersburg Review, 4, 1852, 55-66, 453-474.

122. _____. "Zwingli at Bern." Mercersburg Review,
      6, 1854, 223-257.

123. Bommeli, Ernst. "Huldrych Zwingli während seiner
      Glarnerzeit 1506-1516." Die reformierte Schweiz,
      1952, 7, 209-211.

124. Bornkamm, Heinrich. "Zwingli, Ulrich." Gestalten
      der Reformation. Wuppertal- Barmen, 1967.

125. Bosshard, Gottfried. "Zwingli und die Gegenwart."
      Gemeindeblatt für die Glieder und Freunde der
      Predigergemeinde, December 31, 1918. Nr. 6.

126. Boudriot, Wilhelm. "Huldrych Zwinglis Tod; z.
      400jähr. Gedenktag der Schlacht v. Kappel."
      Echo von Uetliberg. Supplement to the Limmattaler
      Tagblatt, 1931. Nr. 41.

126a. _____. "De tragiek van Kappel. (11 Oct. 1531)."
      Ons godsdienstig Leven, Hoorn, 1931. Nr. 40.

127. _____. "Zwinglis Lebenswerk." Reformierte
      Kirchenzeitung, Wupperthal, 81, 156.

128. _____. "Zwinglis Tod; z. 400jähr. Gedenktag
      der Schlacht v. Kappel. 11 October 1931."
      Solothurner Tagblatt, 1931. Nr. 41.

129. _____. "Zwinglis Werk." Familienkreis, 1931. Nr.
      41. Supplement to the Allg. Anzeiger v. Zürichsee.

#130. Bouvier, A. Calvin et Zwingli. Geneva: Les
      Cahiers de foi et vérité, 1959.

#131. _____. "Ulrich Zwingli d'après ses oeuvres."
      Revue de Théologie et de Philosophie de Lausanne, 49, 80,
      1931, 205-232.

132. _____. "Zwingli, apôtre du christianisme social."
      Christianisme social, 44, October/November 1931,
      291-304.

133.   Brandes. "Ein christlich Lied (Zwinglis Pestlied)."
       Reformierte Kirchenzeitung, Wupperthal, 81, 389.

134.   Brändli, Emil. "Das Zwingli-Museum." Relig.
       Volksblatt, 28, 1897, p. 301 f.

135.   Brändli, Oskar. "Aus den Zwingli-Liedern von
       Oskar Brändli." Schweizerisches Protestantenblatt,
       6, 52, 1883, 438. [*]

136.   _____. "Wie Ulrich Zwingli die christlichen
       Jünglinge ermahnt." Schweizerisches Protestanten-
       blatt, 21, 1898, pp. 209 ff., 219 ff.

137.   _____. "Zwingli als Führer zum Wort Gottes;
       a. 400 Todestag am 11. Okt." Der Hausfreund.
       Supplement to Bülach-Dielsdorfer-Volksfreund,
       1931. Nr. 42.

138.   _____. "Zwingli." Lieder und Sprüche. Basel,
       1907. [*]

139.   _____. "Zwinglis Abschied." Volkskalender der
       reformierte Schweiz, 1932. [*]

140.   Brändly, Willy. "Legenden um Zwingli." ZWA, 8,
       3, 1945, 168-169.

141.   _____. "Wolfgang Pratensis." ZWA, 7, 4, 1940,
       271-272. Also: ZWA, 7, 9, 1943, 596.

142.   _____. "Zu Zwinglis Waffen." ZWA 9, 8, 1952, 489-
       490.

143.   _____. "Zwingli (Huldrych) in Glarus 1506-
       1516." Tat, 1952. Nr. 253.

144.   Brassel, Karl. "Das Vermächtnis des Reformators
       [Zwingli]." By Quidam [Pseudonym for K.B.].
       Zürichsee-Zeitung, 1931. Nr. 236.

145.   Braun, Rudolf. "Zur Militärpolitik Zürichs im
       Zeitalter der Kappeler Kriege." ZWA, 10, 9,
       1958, 537-573.

146.   Brecht, Martin. "Hat Zwingli seinen Brief an
       Matthaus Alber über das Abendmahl abgesandt?"
       Archiv, 58, 1, 1967, 100-102.

19

147. Bremi, Willi. "Zwingli und die Jungen." Kirchenbote für den Kanton Zürich, 1931. Nr. 10.

148. _____. "Zwingli unter den Eidgenossen." Der
Weg des protestantischen Menschen von Luther bis
Albert Schweizer. Zurich: Artemis Verlag, 1953.
38-49.

149. van den Brink, J. N. Bakhuizen. "Bible and
biblical Theology in the Early Reformation."
SJT, 15, 1962, 50-65.

150. _____. "Zwingli, Huldrych." Winkler Prins
Encyclopaedie. Vol. 18. Amsterdam:
Elsevier, 1954. 877.

#151. Brockelmann, Brigitte. Das Corpus Christianum bei
Zwingli. Breslauer historische Forschungen, V.
Breslau: Priebatsch, 1938. [Breslau dissertation].
R: W. Köhler, HZ, 160, 1939.

152. Bromiley, G. W. "Zwingli, Huldreich." Encyclopedia
Britannica. Vol. 23. Chicago: Encyclopedia
Britannica, Inc., 1969. 1026-1027.

153. Bruining, A. "Lutheranismus, römischer Katholizismus
und Zwinglio-Calvinismus in ihrem gegenseitigen
Verhältnis im 16. Jahrhundert." Teylers. Theol.
Tijdschr. 1911, 182-217, 329-360, 447-476.

154. Brunner, Emil. "Zwingli, der Verkünder der Gottes-
herrschaft." Kirchenbote für den Kanton Zürich,
1931. Nr. 10.

155. Bruppacher, H. "Der Familienname Zwingli."
ZWA, 2, 2, 1905, 33-36.

156. _____. "Zwingli und wir." Gemeindeblatt für die
reformierten Kirchgemeinden des Kantons Glarus,
1919. Nr. 1.

157. Bucer, Martin. "Ungedruckte Briefe Bucers vom
Augsburger Reichstage an Zwingli 1530."
Analecta Reformatoria I. Edited by Emil Egil
Zurich, 1899, pp. 45 ff.

158. Büchi, Albert. "Thomas Trübmann." ZWA, 5, 3,
1930, 126-127.

20

159. Bugmann, Kuno. "Zu Zwinglis Gedenkfeier."
     Einsiedler Anzeiger, 1969. Nr. 16.

160. _____. "Zürich und Einsiedeln." Zürichsee-
     Zeitung, 1969. Nr. 13.

161. _____. "Zürich und Einsiedeln; anlässlich der
     Feier '450 Jahre Reformation in Zürich'."
     Maria Einsiedeln, 74, July 69, 346-352.

162. Burckhard, Claus. "Ulrich Zwingli. Beginn der
     Reformation in der Schweiz, 1 Jan 1519."
     Volksrecht, 1969. Nr. 2.

#163. Burckhardt, Abel Eduard. Das Geistproblem bei Huldrych
     Zwingli . Quellen und Abhandlungen zur
     schweizerischen Reformationsgeschichte, VI.
     Leipzig: M. Heinsius, 1932. [Basel dissertation].
       R: W. Köhler, NZZ, 1932. Nr. 1384;
       W. Bremi, ZWA, 6, 1934, 59-60.

164. Burckhardt, Paul. Evangelium und Kriegszeit.
     Basel, 1931. [*]

#165. _____. Huldreich Zwingli: eine Darstellung
     seiner Persönlichkeit und seines Lebenswerke
     Zurich: Rascher and Cie, 1918.
       R: W. Köhler, NZZ, 1918. Nr. 1086.

166. _____. "Die Katastrophe der Zwinglischen Politik."
     Schweizerische Theologische Zeitschrift, 26, 1909.
       R: W. Köhler, ZWA, 12, 1910, 385-386.

167. _____. "Über Zwinglis Predigttätigkeit." Protestant,
     1931. Nr. 15.

168. _____. "Zwinglis Tod." Schweizerisches Protestanten-
     blatt, 1931. Nr. 41. [*]

169. Burckhardt-Biedermann, Th. "Zum Artikel:
     'Aus Zwinglis Bibliothek'." ZWA, 2, 7, 1908, 220-
     221.

170. Bürki, F. "Huldrych Zwingli ein Chronik."
     Schweizer Realbogen, 58, 1932.

#171.   Büsser, Fritz.(Ed.) Beschreibung des Abendmahls-
         streites von Johann Stumpf auf Grund einer
         unbekannt gebliebenen Handschrift. Zurich:
         Verlag Berichthaus, 1960.
              R: R. Pfister, ZWA, 11, 9, 1963, 618-620;
              G. Heer, ZSKG, 56, 1962, 177-178.

#172.   _____. "Das Bild der Natur bei Zwingli."
         ZWA, 11, 4, 1960, 241-256.

173.   _____. "De prophetae officio. Eine Gedenkrede
         Bullingers auf Zwingli." Festgabe Leonhard
         von Muralt. Edited by Martin Haas and Rene
         Hauswirth. Zurich: Verlag Berichthaus, 1970.

#174.   _____. Das katholische Zwinglibild: Von der
         Reformation bis zur Gegenwart. Zurich: Zwingli
         Verlag, 1968.
              R: H. J. Grimm, JCH, 38, December 1969, 535;
              H. Gutknecht, Kirchenbote für den Kanton
              Zürich, 55, January 1969, 4; H. M. Stückelberger,
              ZWA,13,3, 1970, 211-213; H. Jedin, NZZ, 1969.
              Nr. 185.

#175.   _____. "Der Prophet--Gedanken zu Zwinglis
         Theologie." 450 Jahre Zürcher Reformation.
         Special edition of ZWA, 13, 1, 1969. Zurich:
         Buchdruckerei Berichthaus, 1969. 7-18.

176.   _____. "Zum Zwingli-Jubiläum. Hinweise auf
         drei Publikationen." NZZ, 1969. Nrs. 431, 433,
         436.

177.   _____. "Zwingli, die Eidgenossen und das Konzil
         von Trient." NZZ, 1963. Nrs. 4973, 4978.

178.   _____. "Zürich, die Stadt der Reformation
         Huldrych Zwinglis." Das reformierte Zürich.
         Edited by the Kirchenrat des Kantons Zürich,
         1969, 9-11.

179.   _____. "Zwingli und Laktanz." ZWA, 13, 6,
         1971, 375-399.

180.   _____. "Zwingli und die Universität Zürich."
         Mimeographed manuscript distributed on the
         occasion of the 450th anniversary of the
         Zurich Reformation. Zurich, 1969.

181.   _____. "Das Zwingli-Bild von Emil Egli bis Fritz
        Blanke." NZZ, 1969. Nr. 4.

182.   Cadoux, Cecil J. "Zwingli." Christian Worship.
        Edited by Nathaniel Micklem.   Oxford, 1936.
        137-153.

#183.   Calvetti, C. "Presupposti e postulati filosofici
        nel pensiero di Zwingi." Rivista di Filosofia
        neoscolastica, 1957, 25-33.

184.   Campenhausen, H.von"Die Bilderfrage in der
        Reformation." ZKG, 68, 1/2, 1957, 96-128.

185.   _____. "Zwingli und Luther zur Bilderfrage."
        Das Gottesbild im Abendland. Witten and Berlin,
        1959.

186.   Capito, Wolfgang Fabricius. "Ein Brief von ihm vom
        25. September 1530 an Zwingli." Analecta
        Reformatoria I. Edited by Emil Egli. Zurich,
        1899. 60.

187.   Cherbuliez, A. E. "Zwingli, Zwick und der
        Kirchengesang." ZWA, 4, 12, 1926, 353-377.

188.   Christen, Ernest. Zwingli avant la Réforme de
        Zürich Histoire de son developpement intellectuel
        et religieux. Geneva: Romet, 1899. [Geneva
        dissertation].

189.   Claassen, Walter. Die Agrarpolitik Zürichs im
        Zeitalter der Reformation. Jena, 1899.
        [Jena dissertation].

190.   _____. Schweizer Bauernpolitik im Zeitalter
        Ulrich Zwinglis. Ergänzungshefte z. Zeitschrift
        für Sozial- und Wirtschaftsgeschichte, IV.
        Berlin: E. Felber, 1899.

191.   Clay, H. Alexander. "Huldreich Zwingli a man
        1484-1531." Contemporary Review, 140, November
        1931, 629-636.

192.   Clemen, Otto. "Zwingliana in der Bibliothek des
        Gervasius Sopher." ZWA, 5, 7, 1932, 342-243.

23

193.   Clever, C. "Huldreich Zwingli." Reformed
        Church Review, 5, 1901, 303-316.

194.   Corneliussen, C. P. "Ulrich Zwingli." Fyns
        Venstreblad,1931, 8 October.

195.   Corrodi-Sulzer, A. "Die Schlacht bei Kappel und
        das Näfengeschlecht." ZWA, 4, 9, 1925, 276-278.

196.   _____. "War Zwingli Bürger von Zürich?" ZWA,
        4, 14, 1927, 447-448.

197.   _____. "Das Wirtshaus zum Ochsen in Zürich."
        ZWA, 4, 11, 1926, 340-342.

198.   _____. "Zwinglis Vermögensverhältnisse." ZWA, 4,
        6, 1923, 174-188. See also: NZZ, 1923. Nr. 325.

#199.   Courvoisier, Jaques. "Réflexions à propos de la
        doctrine eucharistique de Zwingli et de Calvin."
        Festgabe Leonhard von Muralt. Edited by Martin
        Haas and Rene Hauswirth. Zurich: Verlag
        Berichthaus, 1970. 258-264.

200.   _____. "Vom Abendmahl bei Zwingli." ZWA, 11, 7,
        1962, 415-426.

201.   _____. "Zwingli -- A Christological Theologian."
        Ecumenical Review, 6, April 1954, 342-344.

202.   _____. Zwingli. Geneva: Éditions Labor et Fides,
        1947.

#203.   _____. Zwingli: A Reformed Theologian. Richmond:
        John Knox Press, 1963. See also: Zwingli,
        théologien réformé. Neuchâtel, 1965; Zwingli als
        reformierter Theologe. Translated by R. Pfister.
        Zeugen und Zeugnisse, XI. Neukirchen-Vluyn:
        Neukirchener Verlag des Erziehungsvereins, 1966.
        R: W. Meyer, ZWA, 13, 3, 1970, 218-220;
        G. S. M. Walker, SJT, 21, March 1968, 84-85;
        F. Schmidt-Clausing, ThL, 92, July 1967, 527-9;
        L. M., Verbum Caro, 22, 87, 1968, 102-103;
        C. Dumont, Nouvelle Revue Théologique, 89,
        February 1967, 213; G. Besse, Revue de Théologie
        et de Philosophie, 17, 1967, 71; Margaret Bowker,
        Theology, 68, 1965, 257-259.

24

204. Courvoisier, Jaques. "Zwingli et Karl Barth."
    Antwort, Festschrift zum 70. Geburtstag von
    Karl Barth. Zollikon, Zurich: Evang. Verlag, 1956.
    369-387. See also: Remède de cheval, textes
    publiés à l'occasion du 70ᵉ anniversaire de
    Karl Barth. Edited by Jaques Courvoisier, Jaques de
    Senarclens, W. A. Visser t'Hooft. Les Cahiers
    de Renouveau, XIII. Geneva, 1956. 47-81.
        R: R. Pfister, Archiv, 51, 1960, 152.

205. Cramer, J. A. "Zwingli's sacraments en avondmaals-
    beschouwing." Nieuwe Theologische Studien, 25,
    1942, 61-74.

206. Cristiani, L. "Réforme. X. La Réforme en Suisse."
    Dictionnaire apologétique de la foi catholique.
    Edited by A. d'Alès. Vol. IV. Paris, 1922.
    Cols. 733-737.

207. _____. "Zwingli." Dictionnaire de Théologie
    Catholique. Pt. 13/2. Paris, 1936. Cols. 2020-
    2097. See also: Pt. 14/1. Paris, 1939. Cols.
    441-465. Also: Pt. 15/2. Paris, 1950. Cols.
    3716-3744.

208. Csikesz, Alexander. "Zum Gedächtnis Zwinglis."
    NZZ, 1930. Nr. 1964.

209. Cunz, Dieter. Ulrich Zwingli. Aarau: H. R.
    Sauerländer, 1937.
        R: W. Köhler, Basler Nachrichten, 1937. Nr. 193;
        HZ, 157, 1938; Zeitschrift für die Geschichte
        des Oberrheins, N.F. 52, 1939; L. von Muralt,
        NZZ, 1937. Nr. 1154; G. C. Sellery, AHR, 48,
        1942/43, 181-182.

210. Curtis, W. A. "Confessions: Confessions in the
    Zwinglian (Presbyterian) Churches." Encyclopaedia
    of Religion and Ethics. Edited by James
    Hastings. Vol. III. New York: Charles Scribner's
    Sons, 1955. 857-861.

211. Dändliker, Karl. "Zürcher Volksanfragen von
    1521-1798. 1. Die Volksanfragen in der Zeit
    Zwinglis 1519-1531." Jahrbuch für schweizerische
    Geschichte, 23, 1898, pp. 151 ff.

212. Däster, Adolf. "Ulrich Zwingli." St. Galler
      Tagblatt, 1931. Nr. 476.

213. Davies, Rupert Eric. The Problem of Authority
      in the Continental Reformers: A Study in Luther,
      Zwingli, and Calvin. London: The Epworth
      Press, 1946.

214. Dejung, Emanuel, and Wuhrmann, Willy. Zürcher
      Pfarrerbuch (1519-1952). Zurich: Schulthess &
      Co., 1953.
        R: L. von Muralt, ZWA, 11, 1, 1959, 47-56.

215. Delinotte, Théodore. Ecclésiologie de Zwingli.
      Cahors: A. Coneslant, 1899. [Montauban
      dissertation].

216. Dierauer, Johannes. Geschichte der schweizerischen
      Eidgenossenschaft. Vol. III: 1516-1648. Gotha:
      F. A. Perthes, 1907.
        R: ZWA, 2, 1907, 159-160.

217. Dommann, Hans. "Luzern im 2. Kappelerkrieg;
      z. Gedächtn. der Ereignisse vor 400 Jahren."
      Vaterland, 1931. Nr. 241, 251.

218. Doornkaat, Hans ten. "Zwinglis Kirche --
      Zwinglikirche?" NZZ, 1969. Nr. 4.

219. Dreske, Otto. Zwingli und das Naturrecht. Halle:
      C. A. Kaemmerer, 1911.

220. Drews, Paul. "Die Anschauungen reformatorischer
      Theologen über die Heidenmission. III. Die Schweizer
      Reformatoren. 1. Zwingli." Zeitschrift
      für praktische Theologie, 19, 3, 1897, pp. 217 ff.

#221. Dreyfuss, Heinrich. Der Politiker Ulrich Zwingli
      und die Entwicklung eines politischen
      Gemeinsinns in der Schweizerischen Eidgenossenschaft. Brelau,
      1925. Reprinted in ZSG, 6, 1926, 61-127, 145-
      193.
        R: W. Köhler, HZ, 133, 1926; 136, 1927.

222. Dubbs, Joseph Henry. Leaders of the Reformation.
      Philadelphia: The Heidleberg Press, 1898.

223. Dürrleman, Freddy. "Zwingli d'après Zwingli, 1484-
      1531." La Cause, 1931.

26

#224. Ebeling, Gerhard. "Cognitio Dei et Hominis." Geist und Geschichte der Reformation. Festgabe Hanns Rückert zum 65. Geburtstag. Berlin: Walter De Gruyter & Co., 1966. 271-322. See also: Lutherstudien, Vol. I. By Gerhard Ebeling. Tübingen: J. C. B. Mohr, 1971, 221-272.

225. Eckinger, Armin. "Der Anteil der Gemeinde Küsnacht an der Reformation." Zürichsee-Zeitung, 1931. Nrs. 238, 239.

226. Edelmann, Heinrich. "Die Ammänner Zwingli 'zum Wilden Hus'." ZWA, 11, 3, 1960, 193-197.

#227. Eekhof, A. "Auslegung und Gründe der Schlussreden Zwinglis, durch Ulrich Zwingli zu Zürich am 29. January 1523 erschienen." Troffel en Zwaard, 12, 1909, 1-21, 77-93, 157-173; 13, 1910, 34-42, 92-105, 171-184, 218-240, 287-295; 14, 1911, 292-306.

228. _____. "Zwingli in Holland." ZWA, 3, 12/13, 1918/1919, 370-384.

229. Eells, Hastings. "The correct date for a letter to Zwingli." Revue belge de philologie d'histoire. 1922.
       R: W. Köhler, ZWA, 4, 5, 1923, 156.

230. Egli, Emil. Albrecht Dürer und Zürich." ZWA, 2, 1910, 384-385.

#231. _____. Analecta reformatoria. I. Dokumente und Abhandlungen zur Geschichte Zwinglis und seiner Zeit. Zurich: Zürcher & Furrer, 1899.
       R: W. Köhler, Lit. Zentrablatt, 51, 1900. Nr. 3.

232. _____. "Ein angebliches Bild Zwinglis in Berlin." ZWA, 1, 3, 1898, 48.

233. _____. "Anlässlich des neuen Zwingli-Dramas." ZWA, 2, 1, 1905, 27-29.

234. _____. "Aus dem Badischen." ZWA, 2, 1, 1905, 11-12.

235. _____. "Aus dem Elsass." ZWA, 2, 1, 1905, 12-13.

236.   Egli, Emil. "Aus dem Schwabenland." ZWA, 2,
       1, 1905, 6-11.

237.   _____. "Aus Zwinglis Bibliothek." ZWA, 2, 6,
       1907, 180-184.

238.   _____. "Aus Zwinglis Bibliothek." ZWA, 2, 8,
       1908, 247-249.

239.   _____. "Ein Autograph Zwinglis." ZWA, 1, 7,
       1900, 137-138.

240.   _____. "Bemerkungen über Zwinglis Bild." ZWA, 1,
       2, 1897, 34.

241.   _____. "Eine Berichtigung zu Bullingers
       Reformationsgeschichte." ZWA, 2, 12, 1910,
       381-383.

242.   _____. "Biographien. VI. Gregor Bünzli."
       ZWA, 2, 14, 1911, 444-449.

243.   _____. "Ein biographisches Trümmerfeld."
       ZWA, 1, 17, 1904, 454-457.

244.   _____. Ein Brief von Zwingli aus dem Himmel, 1910.

245.   _____. "Bullingers Beziehungen zu Zwingli."
       ZWA, 1, 16, 1904, 439-443.

246.   _____. "Eine Dedikation Zwinglis." ZWA, 1, 13,
       1903, 351.

247.   _____. "Eine Dedikation Zwinglis." ZWA, 2,
       5, 1907, 158.

248.   _____. "Eine Fürsprache Zwinglis in Bern."
       ZWA, 2, 1, 1905, 1-5.

249.   _____. "Gebet um den rechten Verstand der
       Schrift." ZWA, 1, 5, 1899, 90-91.

250.   _____. "Die 'göttliche Mühle'." ZWA, 2,
       1910, 363-366.

251.   _____. "Ein griechisches Schauspiel an Zwinglis
       Schule." ZWA, 1, 1, 1897, 11-13.

252. Egli, Emil. "Hieronymus Guntius, der Famulus Zwinglis." ZWA, 1, 15, 1904, 401-408.

253. _____. "Ist Bullinger von Zwingli als Nachfolger vorgeschlagen worden?" ZWA, 1, 16, 1904, 443-444.

254. _____. "Eine italienische Schrift wider Zwingli." ZWA, 2, 12, 1910, 384.

255. _____. "Karlstadts Lebensabend in der Schweiz." ZWA, 2, 3, 1906, 77-82.

256. _____. "Lisighaus mit dem Zwinglihaus." ZWA, 2, 2, 1905, 37-38.

278. _____. "Meister Ulrich Funk, Zwinglis Begleiter auf Synoden und Disputationen." ZWA, 2, 1, 1905, 13-17.

279. _____. "Die Neuausgabe der Zwinglischen Werke." ZWA, 1, 15, 1904, 415-416.

280. _____. "Die Neuausgabe der Zwinglischen Werke. Vortrag von E. Egli für den Ferienkurs 1908." ZWA, 2, 9, 1909, 269-278.

281. _____. "Nochmals Zwingli und die Pfarrbücher." ZWA, 1, 6, 1899, 125-126.

282. _____. "Die Pest von 1519 nach gleichzeitigen Berichten." ZWA, 1, 14, 1903, 377-382.

283. _____. "Regula Zwingli, die Tochter des Reformators, Gemahlin Rudolf Gwalthers." ZWA, 1, 13, 1903, 323-329.

284. _____. "Ritter Fritz Jakob von Anwyl, ein thurgauischer Edelmann und Verehrer Zwinglis." ZWA, 2, 2, 1905, 44-51.

285. _____. "Römische Reminiszenzen." ZWA, 2, 2, 1905, 39-44.

#286. _____. Schweizerische Reformationgeschichte. Vol. I: 1519-1525. Edited by Georg Finsler. Zurich: Zürcher & Furrer.
   R: W. Köhler, ZWA, 2, 1909, 317-318; NZZ, 1910. Nr. 123; Theolog. Rundschau, 15, 1912.

287.   Egli, Emil. "Trinkgeschirr." ZWA, 1, 8,
          1900, 182.

288.   _____. "Ulrich Zwingli." Allgemeine deutsche
          Biographie, Vol. 45. Leipzig, 1900. 547-575.

289.   _____. "Von den Reliquien der Zürcher
          Stadtheiligen." ZWA, 1, 15, 1904, 413-415.

290.   _____. "Vorarbeiten für eine Neuausgabe der
          Zwinglischen Werke. 3. Oecolampad an Zwingli,
          4. September (1527)." ZWA, 1, 3, 1898, 45-46.

291.   _____. and Wegeli, Rudolf. "Vorarbeiten für
          eine Neuausgabe der Zwinglischen Werke. 5.
          Zwingli an den Rat zu Diessenhofen, 1. Juni
          1530." ZWA, 1, 4, 1898, 63-64.

292.   _____. "Vorarbeiten für eine Neuausgabe der
          Zwinglischen Werke. 6. Martin Butzer an Zwingli."
          ZWA, 1, 4, 1898, 64.

293.   _____. "Vorarbeiten für eine Neuausgabe der
          Zwinglischen Werke. 7. Humanistennamen in
          Zwinglis Briefwechsel." ZWA, 1, 5, 1899,
          83-84.

294.   _____. "Vorarbeiten für eine Neuausgabe der
          Zwinglischen Werke. 10. Butzer an Zwingli
          (7 ff. August 1530)." ZWA, 1, 6, 1899, 111.

295.   _____. "Vorarbeiten für eine Neuausgabe der
          Zwinglischen Werke. 11. Butzer an Zwingli
          (September 1530)." ZWA, 1, 6, 1899, 111.

296.   _____. "Vorarbeiten für eine Neuausgabe der
          Zwinglischen Werke.12. N. an N. und Capito an
          Zwingli (23. September 1530)." ZWA, 1, 6, 1899,
          111.

297.   _____. "Vorarbeiten für eine Neuausgabe der
          Zwinglischen Werke. 13. Pellican an Zwingli
          (Anfang 1526)." ZWA, 1, 6, 1899, 111-112.

298.   _____. Vorarbeiten für eine Neuausgabe der
          Zwinglischen Werke. 14. Hans von Fuchsstein
          an Zwingli, 15. Januar 1531." ZWA, 1, 6, 1899,
          112-113.

299. Egli, Emil. "Vorarbeiten für eine Neuausgabe
der Zwinglischen Werke. 17. Chronologische
Berichtigungen zum Briefwechsel." ZWA, 1, 8,
1900, 159-160.

300. _____. "Vorarbeiten für eine Neuausgabe der
Zwinglischen Werke. 18. Zu den Briefen Butzers
an Zwingli." ZWA, 1, 9, 1901, 193-194.

301. _____. "Vorfahren und ein Verwandter Zwinglis."
ZWA, 2, 12, 1910, 383-384.

302. _____. "Der Weg zum Gelehrtenberuf." ZWA, 3, 5,
1915, 155.

303. _____. "Die Wellenberg zu Pfungen." ZWA, 1, 5,
1899, 91-94.

304. _____. "Wesen am Walensee und Dekan Bartholomäus
Zwingli." ZWA, 2, 16, 1912, 491-496.

305. _____. "Die zu Baden 'niedergeworfenen' Brief."
ZWA, 2, 12, 1910, 377-381.

306. _____. "Zu Zwinglis Wahl nach Zürich." ZWA,
1, 10, 1901, 223-224.

307. _____. "Zu Zwinglis Kappelerlied." ZWA, 1,
12, 1902, 318.

308. _____. "Zu Zwinglis Porträtbild (Nachtrag)."
ZWA, 1, 11, 1902, 284.

309. _____. "Der Zug der Glarner nach Monza und
Marignano." ZWA, 2, 15, 1912, 484-486.

310. _____. "Zum Piacenzerzug vom Herbst 1521. 1.
Zürcher Reisrodel." ZWA, 2, 3, 1906, 85-88.

311. _____. "Zum Wandkatechismus von 1525." ZWA,
1, 6, 1899, 123-124.

312. _____. "Zur Berner Disputation." ZWA, 2, 1,
1905, 29.

313. _____. "Zur Einführung des Schriftprinzips in
der Schweiz." ZWA, 1, 13, 1903, 332-339.

314. Egli, Emil. "Zur Schlacht von Kappel."
ZWA, 3, 5, 1915, 155.

315. _____. "Die Zürcher Bibel." Zürcher Taschenbuch
auf das Jahr 1895, 1895, 38-77.

316. _____. "Die Zürcherische Kirchenpolitik von
Waldmann bis Zwingli." Jahrbuch für schweizerische
Geschichte, 21, 1896, 3-69. See also: Zürcher
Taschenbuch auf das Jahr 1897.

317. _____. "Zürcherische Schulen vor der Reformation."
ZWA, 1, 9, 1901, 207-210.

318. _____. "Zwei Disticha des Esslinger Schulmeisters
Ägidius Krautwasser (Lympholerius) auf den Tod
Zwinglis." ZWA, 2, 1909, 278-279.

319. _____. "Zwingli als Hebräer." ZWA, 1, 8, 1900,
153-158.

320. _____. "Zwingli als Redner." ZWA, 1, 4, 1898,
61-63.

321. _____. "Zwingli in Monza." ZWA, 1, 15, 1904,
387-392.

322. _____. "Zwingli in Wien." Theologische Zeitschrift
aus der Schweiz, 92, 186.

323. _____. "Zwingli über den Krieg; ein Wort
an die Geistlichen Englands." Protest.
Monatshefte, 4, 5, 1900, 194-197. See Also:
Schweizerisches Protestantenblatt, 23, 1900,
pp. 179 ff.

#324. _____. "Zwingli, Ulrich 1484-1531." Real-
encyklopädie für protest. Theologie und Kirche.
Third Edition. Edited by Albert Hauck. Vol. 21,
774-815.

325. _____. "Zwingli und die Pfarrbücher." ZWA, 1,
5, 1899, 86-90.

326. _____. "'Zwingliana' von 1719." ZWA, 2, 5,
1912, 487.

327. Egli, Emil. "Ein Zwingliautograph." ZWA, 1,
    11, 1902, 284-285.

328. _____. "Ein Zwingli-Autograph." ZWA, 2, 5,
    1907, 157-158.

329. _____. "Ein Zwingli-Autograph." ZWA, 2, 7,
    1908, 224.

330. _____. "Zwinglibriefe in der Schweiz." ZWA,
    2, 6, 1907, 187-189.

331. _____. "Zwingli-Drucke in Paris." ZWA, 2,
    6, 1907, 184.

332. _____. "Das Zwingli-Museum." ZWA, 1, 1, 1897,
    1-2.

333. _____. "Zwinglis Bild." ZWA, 1, 1, 1897, 3-8.

334. _____. "Zwinglis Capperlied nach Johannes
    Kesslers Sabbata." ZWA, 1, 11, 1902, 251-254.

335. _____. "Zwinglis Geburtsdatum." ZWA, 2,
    3, 1906, 74-75.

336. _____. "Zwinglis lateinische Bibel." ZWA,
    1, 6, 1899, 116-120.

337. _____. "Zwinglis Riesensprung." ZWA, 1, 5,
    1899, 85-86.

338. _____. "Die Zwinglischen Werke." ZWA, 2,
    2, 1905, 63-64.

339. _____. "Zwingli-Zili-Tschudi." ZWA, 2, 5,
    1907, 145-147.

340. Ehrenzeller, Wilhelm. "Zur Bedeutung des 11.
    Okt. 1531." St. Galler Tagblatt, 1931. Nr. 476.

341. Eisinger, W. Gesetz und Evangelium bei Huldrych
    Zwingli. Heidelberg, 1957. [Heidelberg
    dissertation].

342. Ekermann, Peter. De Zwingliana per Helvetiam
    reformatione, 1742.

343. Emser, Hieronymus. "Defense of the Canon of the
     Mass (1524)." Unpublished English translation
     by Henry Preble, prepared for Samuel Jackson.
     New York: Union Theological Seminary Library, n.d.

344. _____. "Presbyter Jerome Emser's apologeticon
     in reply to Huldreich Zwingli's antibolon."
     Unpublished English translation by Henry Preble,
     prepared for Samuel Jackson. New York: Union
     Theological Seminary Library, 1904.

345. Entrèves, A. P. d'. "Stato e chiesa secondo
     Zwingli." Riv. intern. di filos. del diritto,
     11, 1931, 490-496.

346. "Epitaphien auf Huldreich Zwingli." ZWA, 2,
     14, 1911, 419-433.

347. Eppler, P. "Die Gedanken der Reformatoren über
     die Frömmigkeit und Seligkeit der Heiden."
     Evangelisches Missionsmagazin, 62, 1918,
     pp. 6 ff., 43 ff.

348. Epprecht, Robert. Ulrich Zwingli. Acht dramatische
     Bilder aus seinem Leben. Zurich, 1931. [*]

349. Erdos, Karl v. "Ein bisher noch ungedruckter
     Brief Zwinglis." ZWA, 2, 16, 1912, 496-500.

350. Erhard, O. "Ein Brief Ulrich Zwinglis an den
     Rat von Kempten vom 6. Marz 1530." ZWA, 4,
     10, 1925, 296-300.

351. Erichson, Alfred. "Der 400jähr. Geburtstag
     Ulrich Zwinglis." Evangel.-protest. Kirchenbote
     für Elsass-Lothringen. 13, 1884, 2.

352. Ernst, Fritz. "Zwingli, der Schöpfer des modernen
     Zürich." Jahrbuch vom Zürichsee, 1944/45, 67-69.

353. "Errinnerungsblätter zur Einweihungsfeier des
     Zwingli-Denkmals in Zürich." Two brochures
     Number 1: "Zwinglis Lebensbild. Geschichte
     des Zwingli-Denkmals." Number 2: "Einweihungs-
     feier des Denkmals. Festreden und Festgedichte."
     Zurich, Zürcher & Furrer, n.d.

34

354.   Escher, Hermann. "Autographen Zwinglis aus
        der Stadtbibliothek Zürich." Theolog. Zeitact.
        aus der Schweiz, II, 217.

355.   _____. "Ein neues Zwinglibild." ZWA, 2, 15, 1912,
        486-487.

356.   _____. "Eine Rechtfertigung Zwinglis wegen übler
        Nachrede gegen Bern." ZWA, 6, 2, 1934, 119-121.

357.   _____. "Das sogenannte Bildnis Zwinglis in den
        Uffizien." ZWA, 1, 8, 1900, 160-161.

358.   _____. "Ulrich Zwingli." Schweizerische
        Illustrierte Zeitung, 1931. Nr. 15.

359.   _____. "Ein verschwundener und wieder zum
        Vorschein gekommener Brief Zwinglis."
        ZWA, 4, 8, 1924, 225-231.

#360.   _____. Zum Gedächtnis der Zürcher Reformation
        1519-1919. Zurich: Buchdruckerei Berichthaus,
        1919.

#361.   _____. "Zwingli als Staatsmann." ZWA, 5,
        5/6, 1931, 297-317.

#362.   _____. "Zwingli und Luther, ihr Streit um das
        Abendmahl in seinen politischen und religiösen
        Beziehungen." ZWA, 4, 8, 1924, 249-255.

363.   _____. "Zwingli-Rede, gehalten in der
        'Gesellsch. f. deutsche Kunst u. Literatur'
        in Genf." NZZ, 1931. Nr. 2290.

364.   _____. "Zwinglis letztes Geisteserzeugnis."
        ZWA, 4, 10, 1925, 312-315.

365.   Escher-Bürkli, J. "Eine Dedikation Zwinglis."
        ZWA, 2, 3, 1906, 93.

366.   Escher, Nanny von. "Zwingli-Heime." NZZ, 1931.
        Nr. 142.

367.   Etter, Paul. "Huldrych Zwinglis 'Rechte Hand:'
        Landvogt u. Bürgermeister Hans Rudolf Lavater,
        1491-1557." Die Reformierte Schweiz, 1951,
        12, 388-391.

35

368. Eucken, Rud. "Zwingli und Calvin." Die Lebens-
      anschauungen der grossen Denker. Leipzig,
      1899. pp. 276 ff.

369. Eulenberg, Herbert. "Ulrich Zwingli; zu sein.
      400. Todestag am 11. Okt. 1931." Neueste
      Nachrichten, Dresden. October 11, 1931.

370. Eya, Jon L. "Zwingli als sozialer Reformator, ein
      Bannerträger für unsere Zeit." Schweizerisches
      Protestantenblatt, 1919. pp. 36 ff., 42 ff.

371. _____. "Zwinglis Botschaft an unsere Zeit."
      Lecture given in Basel Minster on the occasion of
      the 400th anniversary of the death of Zwingli.
      Basel: G. Krebs, 1931.

#372. Fabian, Ekkehart. "Die Institution des zürcher
      Geheimen Rates der Zwingli-Zeit." ZWA, 13, 5,
      1971, 343-364.

#373. _____. "Zwingli und der Geheime Rat 1523-1531."
      Gottesreich und Menschenreich. Ernst Staehelin
      zum 80. Geburtstag. Basel and Stuttgart:
      Verlag Helbring & Lichtenhahn, 1969. 149-195.

374. Faller, H. "Bildersturm?" Volkskalender für
      die reformierte Schweiz und ihre Diaspora, 13,
      1935.

375. Fallet, Eduard M. "Zwingli als Musiker."
      NZZ, 1925, Nrs. 1549, 1556, 1566.

376. Farner, Konrad. "Hat Dürer Zwingli gemalt?"
      Der öffentliche Dienst, 1948. Nr. 38.

#377. Farner, Alfred. Die Lehre von Kirche und
      und Staat bei Zwingli. Tübingen: J. C. B.
      Mohr, 1930.
         R: Zeitschrift der Savigny-Stiftung für
      Rechtsgesch. Kanon, 1931, 20;
      W. Köhler, Basler Nachrichten, 1931. Nr. 208;
      Theolog. Rundschau. N. F. 4, 1932;
      L. von Muralt, ZWA, 5, 7, 1932, 343-345.
      E. Müller, ZSKG, 27, 1933.

378. _____. "Die Schlacht bei Kappel in Beziehung
      auf Bülach." ZWA, 1, 13, 1903, 339-341.

379. Farner, Alfred. "Zu Zwinglis 'Gutachten
im Ittinger Handel'." ZWA, 1, 15, 1904,
398-401.

380. Farner, Oskar. "Anna Reinhart, die Gattin
Ulrich Zwinglis." ZWA, 3, 7/8, 1916, 197-211,
229-245.

381. _____. "Anna Zwingli." Kirchenbote, 14,
February 1928, 12-13.

382. _____. "Ansprache, gehalten an der Basler
Oekolampad-Feier, 24. Nov. 1931, betr.
Verhältnis v. Oekolampad zu Zwingli."
Münsterbote, Basel, 1931. Nr. 4.

383. _____. "Aus dem Tierkatalog Zwinglis."
Kirchenbote, 42, August 1956, 70-72.

384. _____. "Aus Zwinglis Glarner Zeit [Glarus]."
Kirchenbote für den Kanton Zürich, 1944. Nr. 11.

385. _____. "Aus Zwinglis Jugendzeit." Der
Zwingli-Kalender 1934. Basel: Friedr.
Reinhardt, 1934. 58-60.

386. _____. "Aus Zwinglis Kindheit." Lecture to
the Schulgemeinde d. Freien Evangelische
Volkschule. Zurich: Berichthaus, 1943.

387. _____. "Aus Zwinglis Kindheit. Den Vätern
und Müttern zum Reformationssonntag."
Kirchenbote, November 1943, 82-85.

388. _____. "Aus Zwinglis Studentenzeit in Wien."
Der Zwingli-Kalender 1943. Basel: Friedr.
Reinhardt, 1943. 24-26.
R: L. von Muralt, ZWA, 7, 8, 1942, 534.

389. _____. "Die Bekehrung Zwinglis." Junge Kirche,
1936. Nr. 3, 21-22.

390. _____. Die Chronik von Huldrych Zwinglis Sterben.
Zurich: Berichthaus, 1931.
R: W. Köhler, Theolog. Rundschau, N. F. 4,
1932.

391. Farner, Oskar. "Der Fuhrmann Gottes."
      Reformierte Schweiz, 1949, 51-54, 84-92,
      149-152, 181-187. [*]

392. _____. Der Fuhrmann Gottes. Zwingli-Bücherei,
      LVIII. Zurich: Zwingli Verlag, 1949. [*]

393. _____. "Ein Gebet Zwinglis." Reformierte
      Schweiz, 8, 1951, 387.

394. _____. Die grosse Wende in Zürich. Otto
      Münchs Zwingli-Türe am Grossmünster, with
      Hans Hoffmann; photographs by Ernst Winizki.
      Zurich: Zwingli Verlag, 1941.
        R: L. von Muralt, ZWA, 7, 10,
      1943, 635-637.

395. _____. "Huldrych Zwingli." Zurich, 1919.

396. _____. "Huldrych Zwingli." Grosse Schweizer Forscher.[1]
      Zurich: Atlantis-Verlag, 1938, 66-78.

397. _____. "Huldrych Zwingli." Grosse Schweizer
      Forscher. Edited by E. Fueter. Zurich:
      Atlantis-Verlag, 1939. 31-32.

398. _____. "Huldrych Zwingli." Grosse Schweizer Forscher.[1]
      Zurich: Atlantis-Verlag, 1942. 44-45.

399. _____. "Huldrych Zwingli als Persönlichkeit."
      ZWA, 5, 5/6, 1931, 229-242.
        R: W. Kohler, Theolog. Rundschau, N. F. 4, 1932.

400. _____. "Huldrych Zwingli aus Wildhaus (Toggenburg)
      und Zürich, 1484-1531." Grosse Schweizer Forscher.
      Edited by E. Fueter. 2nd ed. Zurich: Atlantic-
      Verlag, 1941. 160.

401. _____. Huldrych Zwingli der schweizerische
      Reformator. Emmishofen: C. Hirsch, 1917.
      2nd ed., 1931.
        R: M. von Knonau, ZWA, 3, 10, 1917, 323-324.

402. _____. Huldrych Zwingli und seine Sprache. Volks-
      bücher des Deutsch-schweizerischen Sprachvereins,
      V. Basel: Ernst Finckh, 1918. 2nd ed.: Erlenbach-
      Zurich: Rentsch, 1931.

[1] Edited by E. Fueter

403.   Farner, Oskar. "Huldrych Zwingli und seine
        Sprache." ZWA, 10, 2, 1954, 70-97.

#404.   _____. Huldrych Zwingli. Vol. I: seine Jugend,
        Schulzeit und Studentenjahre 1484-1506. Zurich:
        Zwingli Verlag, 1943.
        R: O. Weber, ZKG, 66, 1/2, 1954-1955, 187-189;
        L. von Muralt, ZWA, 7, 10, 1943, 637-640;
        L. von Muralt, NZZ, 1943. Nr. 1929.

#405.   _____. Huldrych Zwingli. Vol. II: seine
        Entwicklung zum Reformator 1506-1520. Zurich:
        Zwingli Verlag, 1946.
        R: Rudolf Pfister, ZWA, 8, 9, 1948, 501-511;
        R. H. Bainton, Theology Today, 5, April 1948,
        129-131; A. Rich, Kirchenbote für den Kanton
        Zürich, 1948. Nr. 1. L.v. Muralt, NZZ, 1947, Nr. 608.

#406.   _____. Huldrych Zwingli. Vol. III: seine
        Verkündigung und ihre ersten Früchte 1520-
        1525. Zurich: Zwingli Verlag, 1954.
        R: R. Pfister, ZWA, 10, 2, 1954, 135-141;
        R. Pfister, Kirchenbote für den Kanton Zürich,
        1954. Nr. 20; G. W. Bromiley, JEH, 6, 1955,
        238-239; Fritz Büsser, SZG, 1955, 521-523;
        E. L., N.Winterthurer Tagblatt, 1955. Nr. 46;
        [Vols. I-III]: Ernst Kähler, ThL, 81, 1956,
        cols. 622-624; O. Weber, ZKG, 66, 1954-55,
        187-189.

#407.   _____. Huldrych Zwingli. Vol. IV: Reformatorische
        Erneuerung von Kirche und Volk in Zürich und in
        der Eidgenossenschaft 1525-1531. Edited by
        Rudolf Pfister. Zurich: Zwingli Verlag, 1960.
        R: E. Künzli, ZWA, 11, 4, 1960, 266-271;
        W. A. Schulze, ThZ, 17, Jan/Feb, 1961, 71-72;
        O. Weber, ZKG, 72, 1961, 188-189; E. G. Rüsch,
        HZ,192,1961, 658-660; R. Stupperich, Archiv,
        53, Nr. 1/2, 1962, 254-255; Ernst Kähler, ThL,
        87, 1962, 219; G. Besse, Revue de Théologie et
        de Philosophie, 11, 1961, 280-281.

408.   _____. "Huldrych Zwingli; zur 400. Wiederkehr s.
        Todesjahres." Evangelischer Volksbote, 42, 1931.

409.   _____. "Leo Jud, Zwinglis treuester Helfer."
        ZWA, 10, 4, 1955, 201-209.

410. Farner, Oskar. "Der letzte Privatbrief Zwinglis." Der Zwingli-Kalender 1935. Basel: Friedr. Reinhardt, 1935.

411. _____. "Der letzte Privatbrief Zwinglis." Kirchenbote, 41, January 1955, 12.

412. _____. "Marburg 1529-1929." Lecture given in Grossmünster at Zurich. Zurich: Wanderer-Verlag, 1929.
    R: L. von Muralt, ZWA, 5, 3, 1930, 132-133.

413. _____. "Die Marburger Disputatz anno 1529. Von Uoli Funk erzehlt." Der Zwingli-Kalender 1927. Basel: Friedr. Reinhardt-Verlag, 1927.

414. _____. "Ein mutmassliches Bildnis Huldrych Zwinglis." ZWA, 8, 1949, 497-501.

415. _____. "Eine neuentdeckte Äusserung Zwinglis über den Gemeindegesang." Jahrbuch für Liturgik und Hymnologie, 3, 1957, 130.

416. _____. "Ein neues Zwingli-Bild." Kirchenblatt für die reformierte Schweiz, 1951. Nr. 107.

418. _____. "Der Radikalismus Zwinglis." Reformatio, 3, 9, 1954, 501-514.

419. _____. Der Reformator Huldrych Zwingli, sein Leben und Schaffen. Zwingli Bücherei, LX. Zurich: Zwingli Verlag, 1949.
    R: L. von Muralt, ZWA, 9, 2, 1949, 120.

420. _____. "Ulrich Zwinglis Sprache." Heisst ein Haus zum Schweizerdegen. Tausend Jahre deutsch-schweizerisches Geistesleben. Vol. I, 1939. 488-498.

421. _____. "Was will Zwingli Heute?" Kirchenbote für den Kanton Zürich, 1919. Nr. 1. Also: Schaffhauser Kirchenboten, 1919. Nrs. 3, 4.

422.   Farner,O."Ein wiedergefundenes Autograph Zwinglis."
        ZWA, 6, 8, 1937, 457-458.

423.   _____. "Zwingli als Prediger." Volkskalender für
        die reformierte Schweiz und ihre Diaspora 1952.
        Basel: Krebs, 1952. 66-69.

424.   _____. "Zwingli als Prediger." Kirchenbote, 44,
        April 1958, 37.

425.   _____. "Zwingli als Seelsorger und Beter." Der
        Zwingli-Kalender 1958. Basel: Friedr. Reinhardt,
        1958. 25-28.

426.   _____. Zwingli, the Reformer, His Life and Work.
        Translated by D. G. Sear. New York: Philosophical
        Library, 1952. See Nr. 401

#427.   _____. "Zwingli und sein Werk." ZWA, 3,
        12/13, 1918/1919, 358-370.

428.   _____. "Zwingli Sterben." Volkskalender für
        die reformierte Schweiz, 33, 1955, 29-35.

429.   _____. "Zwingli warnt vor fremdem Gold."
        Kirchenbote, 12, Bettag 1926, 83.

430.   _____. "Die Zwingli-Ausgabe." ZWA, 10, 5,
        1956, 265-267.

431. _____. Das Zwinglibild Luthers. Sammlung
        gemeinverständl. Vorträge u. Schriften aus
        dem Gebiet der Theologie u. Religionsgeschichte,
        CLI. Tübingen: J. C. B. Mohr, 1931;
          R: L. von Muralt, ZWA, 5, 7, 1932, 345;
        W. Köhler, Basler Nachrichten, 1931. Nr. 208;
        Theolog. Rundschau. N.F. 4, 1932; NZZ, 1931.
        Nr. 325; N. Winterthurer Tagblatt,1931. Nr. 40;
        O. E. Strasser, SZG, 1932. Nr. 1.

432.   _____. "Ein Zwinglibrief." Kirchenbote, 3,
        1917, 69-70.

433.   _____. "Ein Zwinglibrief." Kirchenbote, 4,
        August 1918, 54-55.

434.   _____. Zwinglis Bedeutung für die Gegenwart.
        Zurich: Beer & Cie, 1919.

41

#435. Farner, Oskar. "Zwinglis Entwicklung zum
       Reformator nach seinem Briefwechsel bis Ende
       1522." ZWA, 3, 1-6, 1913-1915, 1-17, 33-
       45, 65-87, 97-115, 129-141, 161-180.
       R: W. Köhler, Theolog. Rundschau, N.F. 4,
       1932.

436. _____. "Zwinglis erstes Schweizerlied."
      Der Zwingli-Kalender 1945. Basel: Friedr. Rein-
      hardt, 1945.

437. _____. "Zwinglis häusliches Leben." Ulrich
      Zwingli: Zum Gedächtnis der Zürcher Reformation
      1519-1919. Zurich: Berichthaus, 1919.

438. _____. "Zwinglis Lehre von den Sakramenten
      und vom kirchlichen Amt." Der Kirchenfreund,
      1937, 19, 289-293.

439. _____. "Zwinglis Persönlichkeit." NZZ,
      1931. Nr. 1918. See also: Der Zwingli-Kalender
      1946. Basel: Friedr. Reinhardt, 1932 .

440. _____. "Zwinglis Pesterlebnis." Der Zwingli-
      Kalender 1946. Basel: Friedr. Reinhardt, 1946.
      26-30. See also: NZZ, 1944. Nr. 1916; Tages-
      Anzeiger, 1944. Nr. 262; N. Winterthurer
      Tagblatt, 1945. Nr. 42.

441. _____. "Zwinglis Sprache und Stil." Kirchenbote,
      40, September 1954, 78-79.

442. _____. "Zwinglis Sterben." Kirchenbote, 17, October 1931,
      81-82. Also: Volkskalendar f. die reform. Schweiz, 1955
      29-35.

443. _____. "Zwinglis Waffen." Volkskalender für
      die reformierte Schweiz und ihre Diaspora, 1949,
      56-58.

444. Fast, H. "Dependence of the first Anabaptists
      on Luther, Erasmus, and Zwingli." MQR, 30,
      April 1956, 104-119.

445. _____. "Fritz Blanke's contribution to the
      interpretation of Anabaptism." MQR, 43,
      January 1969, 51-69.

446. Federer, Karl. "Huldrych Zwingli und Mariae Himmelfahrt." Vaterland, 1950. Nr. 261.

447. _____. "Zwingli und die Marienverehrung." ZSKG, 45, 1951, 13-26.

448. Fehr, Karl. "Zwingli und Pindar." NZZ, 1942. Nrs. 1774, 1783.

449. Fehr, Louis. "Ulrich Zwingli als Politiker." Dav. Bürklis Züricher Kalender, 1931.

450. Ferstberger, Karl. "Drei Zwinglilieder für ein Tasterinstrument Zwinglis," 1947. [*]

451. Festgabe des Zwinglivereins zum 70. Geburtstag seines Präsidenten Hermann Escher. Zurich: Zwingliverein, 1927.
    R: W. Köhler, NZZ, 1927. Nr. 1521.

452. Ficker, Johann. "Verzeichnisse von Schriften Zwinglis auf gegnerischer Seite." ZWA, 5, 4, 1930, 152-175.

453. _____. "Zwinglis Bildnis." ZWA, 3, 12/13, 1918/1919, pp. 418 ff., 435.

454. Fietz, H. "Zwinglis Hütte in Wildhaus." ZWA, 1, 3, 1898, 46-47.

455. Figi, Jacques. Die innere Reorganisation des Grossmünsterstiftes in Zürich von 1519 bis 1531. Zurich: Affoltern am Albis, 1951. [Zurich Dissertation]

456. Finsler, Georg. "Berichtigung zu den zwei Artikeln: 'Zwei Disticha des Esslinger Schulmeisters Aegidius Krautwasser auf den Tod Zwinglis;' und 'Lateinisches Gedicht des Gerardus Noviomagers auf Zwinglis Tod.'" ZWA, 2, 13, 1911, 398.

457. _____. "Dedikationen Zwinglis." ZWA, 2, 6, 1907, 189-190.

458. _____. "Epitaphien auf Huldrych Zwingli." ZWA, 2, 1911, 420-433.

459. Finsler, Georg. "Literatur über Zwingli und seine Reformation." ZWA, 1, 11, 1902, 287-290.

460. _____. "'Lombardick; ja, lüg gar dick.' Ein wort Zwinglis." ZWA, 2, 1906, 101-103.

461. _____. "Das Rabögli, ein von Zwingli gespieltes Musikinstrument." ZWA, 1, 9, 1901, 191-193.

462. _____. "Über Caspar Ulenberg: Vita Zwingli." ZWA, 1, 5, 1899, 81-83.

463. _____. Ulrich Zwingli. Zurich: Zürcher & Furrer.

464. _____. "Vorarbeiten für eine Neuausgabe der Zwinglischen Werke. 15. Hat Zwingli die Schrift Suggestio deliberandi etc. verfasst?" ZWA, 1, 6, 1899, 113-115.

465. _____. "Vorarbeiten für eine Neuausgabe der Zwinglischen Werke. 2. Das Pseudonym Conrad Ryss." ZWA, 1, 2, 1897, 28-31.

466. _____. "Zu Zwinglis Bild." ZWA, 1, 4, 1898, 65.

467. _____. "Zwingli und der Kirchengesang." Kirchenblatt für die reformierte Schweiz, 12, 1897, p. 64 f.

468. _____. "Zwingliana." Kirchenblatt für die reformierte Schweiz, 12, 1897, p. 126 f.

#469. _____. Zwingli-Bibliographie. Zurich: Stiftung von Schnyder von Wartensee, 1897. reprint .: Nieuwkoop: B. De Graaf, 1962.

470. _____. "Die Zwinglihütte in Wildhaus." Kirchenblatt für die reformierte Schweiz, 12, 1897, 45.

471. _____. "Das Zwingli-Museum und Verwandtes." Kirchenblatt für die reformierte Schweiz, 12, 1897, p. 39 f.

#472. _____. "Zwinglis Ausschluss von der Wiener Universität im Wintersemester 1498/99." ZWA, 2, 15, 1912, 466-471.

473. Finsler, Georg. "Zwinglis Kurzsichtigkeit."
      ZWA, 3, 3, 1913, 87-89.

474. _____. "Zwinglis Schrift 'Eine Antwort,
      Valentin Compar gegeben' von England aus
      zitiert." ZWA, 3, 4, 1914, 115-117.

475. Finsler, Rudolf. "Wie Zwingli für das Volk
      sorgte." Gemeindeblatt für die Glieder und
      Freunde der Grossmünstergemeinde, 1918. Nr. 6.

476. _____. "Zwingli und die Jugenderziehung."
      Gemeindeblatt für die Glieder und Freunde der
      Grossmünstergemeinde, 1918. Nr. 6.

477. Flach, Henri. Parallèle entre Zwingli et Calvin.
      Strassbourg, 1832.

478. Flachsmeier, Horst Reinhold. Ulrich Zwingli,
      Politiker und Reformator. Zeugen des gegen-
      wärtigen Gottes, CXLIII. Giessen, Basel: Brunnen-Verlag,
      1960.

479. Fleischlin, B. Schweizerische Reformations-
      geschichte. Luzern, 1903.

480. Fluri, Adolf. Egli, Emil. "Die erste Berner
      Synode." ZWA, 1, 7, 1900, 144-145.

481. Fluri, Adolf. "Die französische Ausgabe des
      Zürcher Wandkatechismus von 1525." ZWA, 1,
      2, 1897, 21-28.

482. _____. "Luthers Übersetzung des N. T. und ihre
      Nachdrucke in Basel und Zürich." Schweizer
      Schulblatt, 1922.

483. _____. "Nochmals Trinkgeschirr." ZWA, 1,
      10, 1901, 249.

484. _____. "Der Zürcher Wandkatechismus von 1525."
      ZWA, 1, 11, 1902, 265-271.

485. Forrer, Clara. "Zwinglis Tod, Cantate."
      Blütenschnee, neue Gedichte, 1895. 147-159.[*]

486. Forster, Peter. "'Ecclesia' und 'Magistratus'
      in Zwinglis letzer Schrift. Zu zwei Kapiteln
      aus der 'Professio fidei'." NZZ, 1971. Nr. 400.

487. Foster, Frank Hugh. "Zwingli's Theology, philosophy and ethics." Huldreich Zwingli. By Samuel Jackson. New York: G. P. Putnam's, 1901. pp. 363 ff.

488. Franz, Gunther. "Huldrych Zwingli. 1.i.1485 bis 11. X.1531." Biographisches Wörterbuch zur deutschen Geschichte, 1953, 951-953.

489. Frei, Oskar. "Aus Zwinglis Briefwechsel." Religiöses Volksblatt, 1919. Nr. 6.

#490. _____. "Bibliographie der poetischen Zwingli-Literatur." ZWA, 6, 2, 1934, 121-126.

491. _____. "Freundes- u. Feindesstimmen nach Zwinglis Todes." Zürcher Post, 1931. Nr. 238.

492. _____. "Schriften zur Schweiz. Reformations-geschichte." Religiöses Volksblatt, 1918. Nrs. 38, 39.

493. _____. "Die Zwingliausstellung in Zürich." Religiöses Volksblatt, 1919. pp. 149 ff.

494. _____. "Zwingli-Lieder; Zwingli Dichtungen aus vier Jahrhunderten, gesammelt u. ausgewählt von O.F." Zurich: Wanderer-Verl., 1931. R: L von Muralt, ZWA, 5, 7, 1932, 347.

495. _____. "Zwinglis Hütte." ZWA, 2, 1906, 126.

496. _____. "Zwinglis Predigt." Religiöses Volksblatt. 1919. Nr. 1.

497. _____. "Zwinglis Tod; Bilder aus Huldrych Zwinglis letztem Lebensjahr." Leben und Glauben, 6, 19. See also: Nachrichten von Zürichsee, 1931. Nr. 157; Zürichsee-Zeitung, 1931. Nr. 235; Religiöses Volksblatt, 1931. Nr. 41.

498. _____. "Zwinglis vaterländisches Wirken." Schweizer Heimkalender, 1919, pp. 113 ff.

499. Fretz, Diethelm. "Der Aufmarsch der Zürcher zur Schlacht von Kappel." Zürichsee-Zeitung, 1931. Nrs. 234-236.

46

500. Frey, Adolf. "Die Kappelkämpfer." Volks-
      kalender für die reformierte Schweiz, 1932.

501. _____. "Zwingli beim Aufbruch nach Kappel"
      Zürcher Festspiel 1901. Zurich, 1901. pp. 128-
      139. [*]

502. _____. "Zwingli; Die Kappelerkämpfer; Zwingli;
      Zwingli und die vier Fakultäten." Festkantate
      zur Universitätsweihe in Zürich 1914. Zurich,
      1914. 15-25. [*]

503. Frey, Arthur. "Huldrych Zwingli als Staatsmann."
      Schweizerisches Volksblatt v. Bachtel, 1931. Nr.
      156; Schaffhauser Intelligenzblatt, 1931. Nr.
      238; Thurgauer Tagblatt, 1931. Nr. 238; Anzeiger
      d. Bez. Horgen, October 9, 1931.

504. _____. "Zwingli und die wirtschaftlichen u.
      sozialen Fragen." Der kleine Bund, 1931. Nr. 41;
      Tössthaler, 1931. Nr. 81; Ev.-soz. Worte, 12.
      Nr. 20; Volkszeitung des Bezirks Pfäffikon, 1931.
      Nr. 122.

505. Frick, Joh. "In der Kammeramtsrechnung 1527."
      ZWA, 2, 7, 1908, 223.

506. Fritschel, G. J. "Luther and Zwingli."
      Lutheran Church Review, 1899, pp. 194 ff., 658 ff.

507. Fröhlich, Abraham Emanuel. "Zwingli als Reformator
      des kirchl. Gottesdienstes." Evangl.-protest.
      Kirchenbote für Elsass-Lothringen, 13, 1884,
      pp. 6 ff.

508. Fuchs, Karl. "Die Zwingliausstellung in Zürich."
      Die Schweiz, 1919, pp. 350 ff.

509. Fuchs, P. G. F. "Zwingli als Pastor und von dem
      Pastorenamte." Die Seelsorge in Theorie und
      Praxis, 5. Nr. 3.

510. Fuchs, Walter. "Huldrych Zwingli, 1531-1931."
      Anzeiger von Uster, 1931. Nr. 235.

511. Fueter, Eduard. "Zwinglis Stellung zur Wahl Karls
      V." Der Anteil der Eidgenossenschaft an der
      Wahl Karls V. Basel, 1899. [Basel dissertation].

512.   Fueter, Karl, "Huldrych Zwingli; z. 400.
       Todestag." Volkszeitung des Bezirks
       Pfäffikon, 1931. Nr. 122.

513.   _____. "Zum 11. Okt. 1931." Ostschweiz. Tagblatt
       und Rorschacher Tagblatt, 1931. Nr. 237.

514.   _____. "Zur Erinnerung an Zwinglis Tod."
       Zürcher Post, 1931. Nr. 247.

515.   _____. "Zwingli als Prediger und Erzieher."
       NZZ, 1958. Nr. 4.

516.   _____. "Zwingli-Geist; z. 11. Okt. 1931."
       Bülach-Dielsdorfer Wochenzeitung, 1931. Nr.
       81; Lägern-Bote, 1931. Nr. 81.

517.   _____. "Zwingli-Literatur, von Omega [pseudonym
       for K. Fueter]." NZZ, 1931. Nr. 1932.

518.   _____. "Zwinglis Tod; z. 11. Okt. 1931."
       Schaffhauser Intelligenzblatt, 1931. Nr. 238.
       Tössthaler, 1931. Nr. 81; Zofinger Tagblatt,
       1931. Nr. 235; Grenzpost, Richterswil, October 7,
       1931.

519.   Gäbler, Ulrich. "Ein übersehenes Stück aus
       Zwinglis Korrespondenz." ZWA, 13, 4, 1970,
       227-230.

#520. _____. "Die Zwingli-Forschung seit 1960."
       ThL, July 1971, 482-490.

521.   Gagliardi, Ernst. Geschichte der Schweiz. Vol. I.
       3rd Edition. Zurich, 1936.

522.   _____. "Mitteilungen über eine gefundene
       Quelle zur zürcherischen Reformationsgeschichte.
       (Hans Edlibach)." ZWA, 2, 13, 1911, 407-414.

523.   _____. "Zwinglis Predigt wider die Pensionen.
       5. März 1525." ZWA, 3, 11, 1918, 337-347.

524.   _____. Müller, Hans; Büsser, Fritz. Johannes
       Stumpfs Schweizer- und Reformations-Chronik.
       2 vols. Quellen zur Schweizer Geschichte, N.F. I:
       Basel, 1952, 1953, 1955.

48

525. Gaillard, Paul André. <u>Loys Bourgeoys</u>.
     Lausanne: Imprimeries réunies, 1948.

526. Gamper, Gustav. "Huldrych Zwingli ermahnt."
     <u>Schweizer Heimkalender für 1916</u>. Zurich,
     1915. 109.

527. Ganz, Werner. "Zwingli und unsere Zeit."
     <u>N. Winterthurer Tagblatt</u>, 1939. Nr. 15.

528. Garside, Charles, Jr. "The Literary Evidence
     for Zwingli's Musicianship." Archiv, 48, 1,
     1957, 56-75.

529. _____. "Some attitudes of the major reformers
     toward the role of music in liturgy."
     <u>McCormick Quarterly</u>, 21, November 1967,
     151-168.

#530. _____. <u>Zwingli and the Arts</u>. Yale Historical
     Publications, LXXXIII. New Haven: Yale
     University Press, 1966.
       R: J. W. Barker, <u>American Record Guide</u>, 35,
     December 1968, 329-330; Ernst Rüsch, ZWA,
     12, 10, 1968, 725-726; Thomas W. Hunt,
     <u>Southwestern Journal of Theology</u>, 11, Fall 1968,
     151; R. Stupperich, Archiv, 58, 2, 1967,
     264-265; L. G. McAllister, <u>Encounter</u>, 28,
     Spring 1967, 196; G. W. Bromiley, <u>Journal of
     Religious History</u>, 5, December 1968, 173-176;
     B. Hall, SJT, 21, September 1968, 361-363;
     K. H. Dannenfeldt, <u>Renaissance Quarterly</u>,
     20, 1967, 47-49.

531. _____. "Zwingli, Huldrych." <u>New Catholic
     Encyclopedia</u>. Vol. 14. New York: McGraw-Hill
     Book Co., 1967. 1141-1143.

532. Gasser, Johann Conrad. <u>Vierhundert Jahre Zwingli-
     Bibel 1524-1924</u>. Zurich: Bibelverlag der
     evangelischen Gesellschaft, 1924.
       R: W. Köhler, <u>Sonntagsblatt der Basler Nach-
     richten</u>, 1925. Nr. 15; ThL, 51, 1926, 280;
     Ernst Staehelin, ZKG, 44, 1925, 628-630.

533. _____. "Zur Zwingli-Gedenkfeier vom 18. Okt.
     1931." <u>N.Winterthurer Tagblatt</u>, 1931. Nr. 254.

534. Gasser, Johann Conrad. "Zwingli als Pädagoge."
N. Winterthurer Tagblatt, 1931. Nr. 277.

535. Gauss, Karl. "Die Beziehungen
Zwinglis zu den Pfarrern des Baselgebiets."
ZWA, 3, 12/13, 1918/1919, 385-395.

536. _____. "Ulrich Zwingli und das Baselgebiets."
Basellandschaftl. Zeitung, 1932. Nr. 20.

537. Gerber, Emil. "Zwinglis Bildnis in der
schweizerischen Medaillenkunst." Festgabe Hans
Lehmann. Anzeiger für schweiz. Altert.-kde, N.F.
33, 1/2. See also: NZZ, 1923. Nr. 1587.

538. Gerig, Georg. Reisläufer und Pensionenherren in
Zürich, Ein Beitrag zur Kenntnis der Kräfte,
welche der Reformation widerstrebten. Zurich, 1519-1532,
1947. [Zurich dissertation]

539. Gerok, Karl. "Zum Zwinglitag, 1. Jan. 1884."
Ausgewählte Dichtungen. Stuttgart, 1907. 251.

540. Gerrish, B. A. "Lord's Supper in the Reformed
Confessions." Theology Today, 23, July 1966,
224-243.

541. Gerstberger, Karl. "Drei Zwingli-Lieder für ein
Tasteninstrument." Zurich: Musik Verlag zum
Pelikan, 1947. [*]

542. _____. "Drei Zwingli-Lieder für 4Stimmigen
Männerchor [a capella]." Zurich: Musik Verlag
zum Pelikan, 1947. [*]

543. Geschichte der Schweiz. By Hans Nabholz, Leonhard
von Muralt, Richard Feller and Emil Durr. Vol. I:
Von den ältesten Zeiten bis zum Ausgang des
16. Jahrhunderts. Zurich: Schulthess, 1932.
R: W. Köhler, Zeitschrift für die Geschichte
des Oberrheins, N.F. 48, 1935.

544. Gessner, Georg. "Zwinglis Jugend."Lieder und
Gedichte zur Denkfeyer usw. Zurich, 1818. 3. [*]

545. _____. "Zwinglis Mannheit." Christliche Lieder
zur Feyer der Reformation, 5. [*]

546. Gessner, Georg. "Zwinglis Tod." Christliche
     Lieder zur Feyer der Reformation , 8.[*]

#547. Gestrich, Christof. Zwingli als Theologe.
     Glaube und Geist beim Zürcher Reformator.
     Studien zur Dogmengeschichte und systematischen
     Theologie, XX. Zürich/Stuttgart: Zwingli
     Verlag, 1967.
       R: H. H. Rowley, The Expository Times, 91,
       8, May 1970, 255; J. Rogge, ThL, 94, August
       1969, 607-609; G. Seebas, ThZ, 25, May/June 1969,
       227-229.

548. Geyer, Paul. "Die soziale Schichtung der
     Bürgerschaft." Zürich vom Ausgang des Mittel-
     alters bis 1798. Zurich, 1952.

549. Ghinzoni, P. "Ulrico Zwingli e Francesco II storza,
     1531." Bolletino storico della svissera italiana,
     1893.

550. Giezendanner, Heinrich. "Die Zwinglihütte als
     Baudenkmal." Toggenburgerblätter für Heimatkunde,
     1945, 7, 31-35.

551. Gilg, Otto. "Huldrych Zwingli, gestorben 11.
     Okt. 1531." Christkathol. Hauskalender 1931.
     Basel, 1930.

552. Gitermann, V. "Zum Stadtstaate Zürich." Geschichte
     der Schweiz, 1941.

553. Goeser, Robert James. "Word and Sacrament: A
     study of Luther's Views as Developed in the
     Controversy with Zwingli and Karlstadt."
     Unpublished Ph.D. dissertation, Yale University,
     1960.

554. Goeters, J. F. Gerhard. "Ein Auszug aus Zwinglis
     'In Catabaptistarum Strophas Elenchus' als
     antitäuferisches Flugblatt." ThZ, 9, 1953,
     395-397.

555. Goguel, Georges-Frédéric. La Vie d'Ulric Zwingli réformeteur. Paris, 1841.

556. Goldschmid, Th. "Evangelische Märtyrer aus
     Zwinglis Zeit und ihre Lieder." Evangelisches
     Schulblatt, 104, 1, January 1969, 9-12.

557. Goldschmid, Th. "Die Lieder Huldreich Zwinglis." Der evang. Kirchenchor, 22, 3; 23, 1/2. R: W. Köhler, ZWA, 3, 16, 1920, 528-529.

558. _____. "Ulrich Zwinglis Kappelerlied." Kirchenblatt für die reformierte Schweiz, 3, 1898, pp. 167 ff.

559. _____. "Zwinglis 'Kappeler-Lied'." Zurich: Hug, 1931. [*]

560. Gollwitzer, Helmut. "Zur Auslegung von Joh. 6 bei Luther und Zwingli." In memoriam Ernst Lohmeyer. Stuttgart, 1951.

561. Good, James I. "The antistes of Zurich." Presbyterian Reformed Review, October 1895.

562. _____. History of the Swiss Reformed Church Since the Reformation. Philadelphia, 1913.

563. _____. The Reformed Reformation. Philadelphia: The Heidelberg Press, 1916. R: F. W. Loetscher, Princeton Theological Review, 20, 1922, 139-142.

564. _____. "Ulrich Zwingli." Address delivered at the World's Sunday School Convention in Zurich. Zurich: F. Amberger, 1913.

565. Gottschick, J. "Hus', Luther's und Zwingli's Lehre von der Kirche." ZKG, 8, pp. 345 ff., 543 ff.

566. Grimm, Harold J. "Zwingli, Huldreich." Twentieth Century Encyclopedia of Religious Knowledge. Edited by Lefferts A. Loetscher. Grand Rapids, Michigan: Baker Book House, 1955. 1204-1205.

567. Grob, August. Huldreich Zwingli, der Reformator und Patriot. Zurich: Beer & Cie, 1913.

568. Grob, Paul. "Zum Todestage Zwinglis." N. Bundner Zeitung, 1931. Nr. 238.

569. Grob, Rudolf Ernst. "Zu Zwinglis Todestag, 11. Oktober, 1531." Schweizer Evangelist, 1931. Nr. 41.

570. Grubenmann, Rudolf. "Die Geister von Kappel." Gebets- und Andachtsbuch für das christliche Volk. Zurich: 1923. p. 181 f.

571. Güder, Emil. "Ulrich Zwinglis Kappelerlied." Kirchenblatt für die reformierte Schweiz,13, 1898, 168.

572. Guggenbühl, Ernst. "Die Ursachen der Niederlage von Kappel." Kirchl. Gemeindebl. für Fischenthal, 1931. Nr. 73.

573. Guggisberg, Kurt. "Lateinische Sprüche über Zwingli." ZWA, 6, 4, 1935, 238-239.

574. _____. "Das Leben Zwinglis und das 'Leben Jesu' von David Friedrich Strauss." ZWA, 6, 4, 1935, 236-238.

#575._____. Das Zwinglibild des Protestantismus im Wandel der Zeiten. Quellen und Abhandlungen zur schweizerischen Reformationsgeschichte, N.F. VIII. Leipzig: M. Heinsius Nachfolger, 1934.
    R: W. Köhler, HZ, 152, 1935; W. Köhler, Basler Nachrichten, 1935. Nr. 108: H. Escher, ZWA, 6, 3, 1935, 189-190. H. Bouché, Das christliche Welt, July 1, 1935. Nr. 13

#576. _____. Das Zwinglibild des Protestantismus von der Reformationszeit bis zur Aufklärung. Bern, 1934.   Gräfenhainichen: A. Heine, 1935. [Bern dissertation].

#577. Gut, Walter. "Zwingli als Erzieher." ZWA, 6, 6, 1936, 289-306.

#578. Gyenge, Landessuperintendent. "Zwingli -- der Sozialrevolutionär." Reformiertes Kirchenblatt, 46, March 1969, 7.

#579. Haas, Martin. Huldrych Zwingli und seine Zeit: Leben und Werk des Zürcher Reformators. Zurich: Zwingli Verlag, 1969.
    R: F. Büsser, NZZ, 1969. Nr. 433.

#580. _____. "Täufertum und Volkskirche -- Faktoren der Trennung." ZWA, 13, 4, 1970, 261-278.

#581. Haas, Martin. Zwingli und der Erste Kappelerkrieg.
       Zurich: Berichthaus, 1965.
         R: W. F. Bense, Journal of Ecumenical Studies,
         6, Winter 1969, 90; R. Stupperich, Archiv,
         58, 1967, 265; Paul Herzog, ZSKG, 60, 1966,
         315-317.

#582. _____. "Zwingli und der Erste Kappelerkrieg.
       Die Streitigkeiten zwischen katholischen   und
       reformierten Orten."   ZWA, 12, 2, 1964, 93-136.

#583. _____. "Zwingli und die 'Heimlichen Räte.'"
       ZWA, 12, 1, 1964, 35-68.

 584. _____. "Zwinglis Stellung in der zürcherische
       Politik zur Zeit der kappeler Kriege."
       Der Landbote, 1962. Nr. 283. See also: N.
       Winterthurer Tagblatt, 1962. Nr. 285.

#585. Hadorn, Wilhelm. Die deutsche Bibel in der
       Schweiz. Die Schweiz im deutschen Geistesleben,
       XXXIX. Leipzig: Haessel, 1925.
         R: W. Kohler, HZ, 134. 1926.

 586. _____. Kirchengeschichtler reformierten Schweiz.
       Zurich: Schulthess, 1908.
         R: W. Köhler, Theolog. Rundschau, 15, 1912.

 587. _____. Männer und Helden. Die schweizerische
       Reformation und ihre Segnungen. Bern: Grunau,
       1917.
         R: W. Köhler, ThL, 42, 1917, col. 390;
         W. Köhler, Theolog. Rundschau, 20, 1917.

 588. _____. Die Reformation in der deutschen
       Schweiz. Die Schweiz in deutschen Geistesleben,
       LIV. Frauenfeld: Huber & Co., 1928.
         R: W. Köhler, Theolog. Rundschau, N.F.4,
         1932; L. von Muralt, ZWA, 5, 3, 1930, 132.

 589. Hagenbach, Karl Rudolf. "Das Friedensmahl
       bei Kappel 1529." Gedichte, Vol. I. Basel, 1846.
       284-287. [*]

 590. Haller, E. A. "Die Stellung unserer Reformatoren
       zur Zins- und Wucherfrage." Katholische
       Schweizerblätter, 17, 1899, pp. 446 ff.

54

591. Hammer, Wolfgang. "Zwinglis Gott und der moderne Geist." Tat, 1969. Nr. 1.

592. Häne, J. Militärisches aus dem Alten Zürichkrieg zur Entwicklungsgeschichte der Infanterie. Zurich, 1928.

593. _____. "Zürcher Militär und Politik im Zweiten Kappelerkrieg." Jahrbuch für schweizerische Geschichte, 38, 1913, 1-72.

594. Hartog, H. H. de. Grosse Dogmatiker: Zwingli. Baarn, Hollandia-Druckerei, o. J.

595. Hase, K. von. "Huldreich Zwingli." Die Furche, 1920, 1.

596. Hasler, Theodor. "Diener und Kämpfer; z. 400. Todestag Zwinglis." Zürcher Volkszeitung, 1931. Nr. 238.

597. _____. "Das letzte Wort [Zwinglis: Was tut's? Den Leib könnten sie töten, nicht aber die Seele," nach Mykonius]; z. 400. Todestag Zwinglis." Anzeiger a. d. Bezirk Affoltern, 1931. Nr. 116; Nachrichten vom Zürichsee, 1931. Nr. 157; N. Winterthurer Tagblatt, 1931. Nr. 236; Werdenberger u. Obertoggenburger, 1931. Nr. 119; Sihlthaler, 1931. Nr. 81; Glarner Nachrichten, 1931. Nr. 236; Oberthurgauer, October 10, 1931.

598. _____. "Zwinglis Erbe." Zürichsee-Zeitung, 1931. Nr. 236.

599. Hauri, E. "Zwingli-Bücher für die Gemeinde." Kirchenbote für die evangelisch -reformierten Kirchen Basel-Stadt, Glarus, Schaffhausen und der Diaspora der Zentral Schweiz und im Kanton Solothurn, January 1969, 1, 3.

600. Hauri, Johannes Rudolf. Die Reformation in der Schweiz im Urteil der neueren schweizerischen Geschichtsschreibung. Schweizer Studien zur Geschichtswissenschaft, N.F. VII. Zurich: Verlag A.G. Gebr., Leemann & Co., 1945.

601. _____. "Vom evangelischen Kirchenlied. II. Huldrych Zwingli." Protestant, 34. Nr. 20.

602. Hauri, Johannes Rudolf. "Zwinglis erste Predigttätigkeit in Zürich." Kirchliches Gemeindeblatt
   Wollishofen, 1919. Nr. 1.

602a. Hausamman, Susi. "Die Textgrundlage von Zwinglis
   'Fidei expositio'." ZWA, 13, 7, 1972, 463-472.

#603. Hauswirth, Rene. "Landgraf Philipp von Hessen
   und Zwingli. Ihre politischen Beziehungen
   1529/1530." ZWA, 11, 8, 1962, 499-552.

604. _____. Landgraf Philipp von Hessen und Zwingli;
   ihre politischen Beziehungen 1529-1530. Zurich,
   1963. [Zurich dissertation]

605. _____. Landgraf Philipp von Hessen u. Zwingli;
   ihre politischen Beziehungen von 1529-1530.
   Teildruck der Phil. I Dissertation. Universität
   Zürich. Zurich: Berichthaus, 1963.

#606. _____. Landgraf Philipp von Hessen und Zwingli.
   Voraussetzungen und Geschichte der politischen
   Beziehungen zwischen Hessen, Strassburg,
   Konstanz, Ulrich von Württemberg und der
   reformierten Eidgenossenschaft, 1526-1531.
   Schriften zur Kirchen- und Rechtsgeschichte,
   XXXV Tübingen: Osiandrische Buchhandlung:
   Basel: Basileia-Verlag, 1968.
     R: E. Rieser, ZWA, 13, 2, 1969, 149-160.

607. _____. "Um Herkunft und Datierung der Kundschaft
   über 'doctor Fabri'." ZWA, 12, 4, 1965, 248-253.

608. _____. "Zur politischen Ethik der Generation
   nach Zwingli." ZWA, 13, 5, 1971, 305-342.

609. _____. "Die Zürcher Obristmeister (Oberst-
   zunftmeister) 1518-1547." ZWA, 7, 8, 1967, 596-602.

610. Heer, Albert. "Zwingli und die Armenfürsorge."
   Zolliker Bote, 1931. Nrs. 40, 41.

611. _____. "Zwinglis Waffen." Zolliker Bote, 1931.
   Nr. 46.

612. Heer, Fridolin. Huldrych Zwingli. Basel, 1918. [*]

613. Hegg, Peter. "Die Drucke der 'Göttlichen Mühle'
   von 1521." Schweiz. Gutenbergmuseum, 1954, 4,
   135-150.

614. Hegi, Friedrich. "Dokumente der altgläubigen
     Chorherrenpartei am zürcherischen Grossmünster."
     ZWA, 2, 1912, 472-484.

615. _____. "Die Schlacht bei Kappel und das Näfen-
     geschlecht." ZWA, 3, 7, 1916, 211-222.

616. Heinzelmann, Siegfried. Tut etwas Tapferes.
     Aus dem Leben des Reformators Huldrych Zwingli.
     Neuffen: Sonnenweg Verlag, 1968.

617. Helbling, P. Leo, O.S.B. "Dr. Johann Fabri und
     die Schweizerische Reformation." Beilage zum
     Jahresbericht der Stiftsschule Einsiedeln, 1932-
     1933. See also: Einsiedeln: Benziger, 1933.
     [Dissertation Freiburg (Switzerland)].

618. Heman, Richard. Mysterium Sanctum Magnum. Um die
     Auslegung des Abendmahls. Zwingli? Calvin? Luther?
     Rom? Luzern: Räber, 1937.

619. Hemmann, Carl. "Zwinglis Stellung zur Tauffrage im
     literarischen Kampf mit den Anabaptisten."
     Schweizerische Theologische Zeitschrift, 36,
     1919, 29-33, 79-85.

620. Henggeler, P. R. "Eine Parodie des Te Deums
     auf Zwingli." ZSKG, 21, 1927, 232-233. [*]

621. Herding, Wilhelm. Die wirtschaftlichen und
     sozialen Anschauungen Zwinglis. Erlangen, 1917.
     [Erlangen dissertation].

622. Hess, Gustav. "Die geschichtliche Entwicklung
     der kirchlichen Gesetzgebung im Kanton Zürich."
     Zürcher Taschenbuch auf das Jahr 1945. Zurich,
     1945. 145-166.

623. Heusser-Schweizer, Meta. "Zur Einweihung von
     Zwinglis Denkmal, den 11. Okt. 1838, I und
     II." Gedichte, Lieder einer Verborgenen.
     Leipzig, 1858. 185-192. 2nd edition: 1863,
     199-202. [*]

624. Hildebrandt, Walter. "Huldrych Zwinglis Bedeutung
     für Volk und Staat." Bülach-Dielsdorfer
     Wochenzeitung, 1931. Nr. 81.

625. Hillerbrand, Hans J. "The Origin of 16th-century
      Anabaptism: another look." Archiv, 53,
      1/2, 1962, 152-180.

#626. _____. "Zwingli's Reformation Turning-point."
      Bibliothèque d'Humanisme et Renaissance,
      31, 1969, 39-46.

627. Hitz, Heinrich. "Eine Dankesschuld an Zwingli;
      Autorreferat über die Zwingli-Festnummer des
      'Freisinnigen'." Der Freisinnige, 1931. Nr. 236.

628. _____. "Ulrich Zwingli, ein Reformationsbild." Bilder
      a. d. Geschichte des Christentums. Karlsruhe,
      1873. pp. 141 ff.

629. _____. "Zwinglis Bedeutung einst und jetzt."
      Der Freisinnige, 1931. Nr. 236.

630. Höchstetter, Wilhelm. Ulrich Zwingli. Karlsruhe:
      G. Braun'sche Hofbuchhandlung, 1873.

631. Hoffmann, Hans. "Ein mutmassliches Bildnis
      Huldrych Zwinglis [von Albrecht Dürer]."
      ZWA, 8, 1948, 497-501.

632. Hoffmann, Hermann. "Ulrich Zwinglis Tod."
      Oberländer Sonntagsblatt, 1931. Nr. 41.

633. Högger, Paul. "Zum Gedächtnis Zwinglis."
      A sermon preached in Grossmünster in Zurich,
      October 11, 1931. Zurich: Beer, 1931.

634. _____. "Zwingli als Politiker." Kirchenbote
      für den Kanton Zürich, 1931. Nr. 10.

635. Hollenweger, Walter J. "Die ausstehende Reformation.
      Zur Verbindlichkeit von Zwinglis Gottesdienst-
      modell." NZZ, 1969. Nr. 4.

636. _____. "Die Reformation." Evangelisches
      Schulblatt, 104, 1, 1969, 3-9.

#637. _____. "Zwingli writes the Gospel into his world's
      agenda." MQR, 43, January 1969, 70-94.

638. Holzhalb, David. "Zur Eröffnung des Zwingli-
      Museums." Zurich, 1899. [*]

639. Horsch, John. "The Struggle between Zwingli and the Swiss Brethren in Zurich." MQR, 7, 1933, 142-161.

640. Hottinger, Johann Jakob. The Life and Times of Ulric Zwingli. Translated by T. C. Porter. Harrisburg, 1856.

641. _____. "Zwinglis Waffen: Lebensbeschreibung des Schweiz. Reformators Ulrich Zwingli." Zwinglis Waffen; and Zwingli-Album. Zurich, 1884.[*]

642. Howorth, Sir H. H. "The Origin and Authority of the Biblical Canon, According to the Continental Reformers: II. Luther, Zwingli, Lefevre and Calvin." Journal of Theological Studies, 9, 1907-1908, 188-230.

643. Huber, Max. Natürliche Gotteserkenntnis. Ein Vergleich zwischen Thomas von Aquin und Huldrych Zwingli. Bern: P. Haupt, 1950.

644. _____. "Von göttlicher und menschlicher Gerechtigkeit." ZWA, 9, 2, 1949, 59-68.

645. Huber, Walther. "Ulrich Zwingli 1519-1919." Thurgauer Zeitung, 1919. Nr. 2.

646. Hug, Henri. "Hommage au réformateur Zwingli." Messager social [de l'Église protestant], 1931. Nr. 14.

647. _____. "La mort de Zwingli." Messager paroissial des Pâquis, Prieuré-Sécheron, 1931. Nr. 10.

648. _____. "La Mort de Zwingli et la politique confessionnelle." Journal de Genève,1931. Nr. 281.

649. _____. "La mort du réformateur Ulrich Zwingli." Almanach Jean Calvin, 1932.

650. _____. "Quelques échos de Cappel." Semeur vaudois, 1931. Nr. 41.

#651. _____. Ulrich Zwingli 1484-1531. Lausanne: La Concorde, 1931.
    R: W. Köhler, Basler Nachrichten, 1931. Nr. 208; W. Köhler, NZZ, 1931. Nr. 2018; L. von Muralt, ZWA, 5, 7, 1932, 345-347.

652. Hug, Henri. "Zwingli, L'ami des jeunes." Messager paroissial des Pâquis, Prieuré-Sécheron, 1931. Nr. 3.

653. _____. "Zwingli et la lutte contre les anabaptistes." Le Protestant de Genève, 1931. Nr. 3.

654. Hugelshofer, Walter. "Ein neues Zwingli-Portrait." NZZ, 1930. Nr. 82; 1931. Nr. 1780.

#655. "Huldrych Zwingli zum Gedächtnis seines Todes am 11. Okt. 1531." ZWA, 5, 5/6, 1931, 227-317.

656. "Huldrych Zwingli zum Gedenken." Werdenberger Obertoggenburger, 100, 13, 1969, 1.

657. Humbel, Frida. "Ein Gedicht gegen Zwingli aus dem Jahre 1526." ZWA, 2, 13, 1911, 400-406.
    R: G. Bossert, ThL, 1912. Nr. 14; W. Köhler, ZWA, 3, 1, 1913, 27.

#658. _____. Ulrich Zwingli und seine Reformation im Spiegel der gleichzeitigen, schweizerischen volkstümlichen Literatur. Quellen zur schweizerischen Reformationsgeschichte, N.F. I. Leipzig: M. Heinsius, 1912.
    R: W. Köhler, ZWA, 2, 1912, 511-512; W. Köhler, NZZ, 1913. Nr. 30; O. Clemen, ZKG, 33, 1912, 614-615.

659. Hunt, R. N. Carew. "Zwingli's theory of Church and State." Church Quarterly Review, 112, 1931, 20-36.

660. Hürlmann, Friedr. J. "Predigt bei der dritten Säkularfeier der Schlacht auf dem Gubel." Zug, 1831.

661. Hüssy, Hans. "Aus der Finanzgeschichte Zürichs in der Reformationszeit. Die neuen Ämter." ZWA, 8, 6, 1946, 341-365.

662. _____. Das Finanzwesen der Stadt Zürich im Zeitalter der Reformation. Affoltern a. A. 1946 [Zurich dissertation].

663. Hyma, Albert. "Hoen's Letter on the Eucharist and
     its Influence upon Carlstadt, Bucer and Zwingli."
     Princeton Theological Review, 24, January
     1926, 124-131.

#664. Jackson, Samuel. Huldreich Zwingli. New York:
     G. P. Putnam's, 1901.
         R: W. Köhler, ThL, 27, 1902, col 403;
         The Independent, 53, 1901, Nr. 2735, 1020-
         1021; Emil Egli, ZWA, 1, 9, 1901, 211-213.

#665. Jacob, Walter. Politische Führungsschicht und
     Reformation, Untersuchungen zur Reformation in
     Zürich 1519-1528. Zurich: Zwingli Verlag,
     1970. [Zurich dissertation]
         R: R. Hauswirth, ZWA, 13, 4, 1970, 254-260.

#666. _____. "Zwingli und 'der' Geheime Rat.
     Entgegnung an Ekkehart Fabian." ZWA, 13,
     4, 1970, 234-244.

667. Jedin, Hubert. "Ulrich Zwingli." Lexikon für
     Theologie und Kirche, 10. Freiburg, 1938.
     1114-1118.

668. Jenny, Beatrice. "Zwinglis Briefwechsel; ein
     Zeitbild." Der Grundriss, 1943, 10/11,
     273-294.

669. Jenny, Markus. Die Einheit des Abendmahlsgottes-
     dienstes bei den elsässischen und schweizerischen
     Reformatoren. Studien zur Dogmengeschichte und
     systematischen Theologie, XXIII. Zurich:
     Zwingli Verlag, 1968.
         R: Martin Brecht, ZKG, 82, 1971, 129-130.

670. _____. "Ergänzungen zur Liste der Zürcher
     Gesangbuchdrucke im Reformationsjahrhundert."
     ZWA, 13, 2, 1969, 132-143.

671. _____. Geschichte des deutsch-schweizerischen
     evangelischen Gesangbuches im 16. Jahrhundert.
     Basel, 1962.
         R: H. Werthemann, ThZ, 18, 1962, 448-449;
         V. S. Leupold, Lutheran Quarterly, 16,
         February 1964, 78; B. Moeller, Archiv, 54, 2,
         1963, 262-264; K.von Fischer, Reformatio, 12,
         February 1963, 123-124; G. Krause, Theol.
         Rundschau, 30, 2/3, 1964, 269-272.

672. Jenny, Markus. "Spott- und Trauermusik auf
      Zwingli am Kasseler Hof." ZWA, 10, 4, 1955,
      216-217.

673. _____. "Zwingli-Epitaphe." ZWA, 10, 4, 1955,
      258-260.

674. _____. "Das Zwingli-Lied in Königsberg."
      ZWA, 13, 2, 1969, 97-160.

675. _____. "Zwinglis mehrstimmige Kompositionen.
      Ein Basler Zwingli-Fund." ZWA, 11, 3, 1960,
      164-182.

#676. _____. Zwinglis Stellung zur Musik im Gottesdienst.
      Schriftenreihe des Arbeitskreises für evangelische
      Kirchenmusik, III. Zurich: Zwingli Verlag, 1966.
         R: Ernst Rüsch, ZWA, 12, 10, 1968, 725-726.

677. Jeschke, J. B. Huldrych Zwingli, Počet z víry a Výklad víry,
      Dva vyznavačské listy curyšského reformatora.
      Kalich-Praha, 1953.

678. Joss, Walter. "Zwingli und Bern." Der Säemann,
      1931. Nrs. 10, 11.

679. Jost, G. "Zwingli und Graubünden." Der Kristall,
      1931. Nr. 1.

680. "Journée de Zwingli." Semaine religieuse, 4, 1919,
      1.

681. Journet, Charles. L'esprit du protestantisme
      en Suisse. Paris: Nouvelle Librairie Nationale,
      1925.

682. "Jubilée de Zwingli." Semaine religieuse, 4,
      1919, 2-4.

683. Kaiser, Julius. "Bij den 400. sterfdag van
      Huldrych Zwingli." Ons godsdienstig Leven, Hoorn,
      1931. Nr. 40.

684. Kambli, Wilhelm. "Der sterbende Zwingli."
      Rel. Volksblatt, 1913, 41, 325.

685. Kammerer, J. "Ein Spottlied auf Zwingli."
      ZWA, 6, 5, 1936, 281. [*]

62

686. Kappus, Adolf. "Ulrich Zwinglis Ende."
Die Wartburg, 1931. Nr. 10.

687. Karrer, Otto. "Zwingli und die Mariologie."
NZZ, 1950. Nr. 2546.
R: Karl Federer, NZZ, 1950. Nr. 2695.

688. Kawerau, G. "Luthers Stellung zu den Zeitgenossen
Erasmus, Zwingli und Melanchthon."
Deutsch-evangelische Blätter, 31, N.F. 6, 1-3.
R: O. Clemen, ZKG, 27, 1906, 378.

689. Keller, Hans. "Huldreich Zwingli, 1484-1531."
Volksblatt a. d. Bezirk Andelfingen, 1931.
Nr. 80/81.

690. _____. Hutten und Zwingli. Berner Untersuchungen
zur allg. Geschichte, XVI. Aarau: H. R.
Sauerlander & Co., 1952.

691. _____. "Die Schlacht bei Kappel 'nach Hans
Edlibach'." Jahrheft der Antiquar. Ges. Hinwil,
1932. Nr. 4.

692. _____. "Das Weinland und die Schlacht bei
Kappel." Volksblatt a. d. Bezirk Andelfingen,
1931. Nr. 85.

693. _____. "Zwinglis Lebensgang--Zwinglis Persönlichkeit." Der Freisinnige, 1931. Nr. 236.

694. Keller, Jacob. "An mein Schweizervolk! Zur
400jähr. Gedenkfeier Zwinglis." Kappel, 1931.

695. Kesselring, H. "Zur Erklärung und Zeitbestimmung
der Gedichte Zwinglis vom Ochsen und vom
Labyrinth." ZWA, 1, 12, 1902, 294-312.

696. Kessler, Joh. "Ueberlieferung des Zwingliliedes."
Monatschrift für Gottesdienst und christl.
Kunst, 1902.

697. Kilchenmann, Küngolt. Die Organisation des
zürcherischen Ehegerichts zur Zeit Zwinglis.
Quellen und Abhandlungen zur Geschichte des
Schweizer. Protestantismus, I. Zurich, 1946.
R: F. Büsser, ZWA, 9, 8, 1952, 496.

63

698. Kirchhofer, H. "Zwingli sagt uns nichts mehr." Kirchenbote für die evangelisch-reformierten Kirchen Basel-Stadt, Glarus, Schaffhausen und der Diaspora der Zentralschweiz und im Kanton Solothurn, January 1969, 1, 3.

699. "Klaglied der Zürcher umb iren erschlagenen Zwingli und schmähung wider die Catholischen mense Octobri 1531." Das deutsche Kirchenlied der Schweiz im Ref. Zeitalter. Edited by Theodor Odinga. pp. 135 ff. [*]

700. Klassen, Peter. "Zwingli and the Zurich Anabaptists" Gottesreich und Menschenreich. Ernst Staehelin zum 80. Geburtstag. Basel and Stuttgart: Verlag Helbing & Lichtenhahn, 1969. 197-210.

701. Kläui, Paul. "Notizen über Gegner der Reformation in Zürich." ZWA, 6, 10, 1938, 574-580.

702. Klauser, Walter. "Zwinglis Pädagogik." Schweiz. Lehrerzeitung, 76. Nr. 41.

703. Klein, Elise. "Anna Reinhard, die Gattin des Zürcher Reformators." Feierabend, 1931. Nr. 42. Supplement to the Emmentaler Nachrichten.

704. Klingenberg, A. "Kapital und Arbeit bei Zwingli." Mittlgn. d. Studienkomm. für soz. Arbeit [des] Schweiz. Reform. Pfarrvereins, May 1932.

705. Knittel, A. L. "Zwinglis Sterben." Evang. Kirchenblatt für den Kanton Thurgau, 1931. Nr. 10.

706. Knonau, Gerold Meyer von. "Bilder aus der schweizerischen Reformations-Geschichte zum 400jährigen Reformations-Jubiläum 1517." ZWA, 3, 9, 1917, 288.

707. _____. "Über eine neueste Beurteilung der Zwinglischen Reformation." ZWA, 2, 8, 1908, 243-245.

708. _____. "Zürich in Jahre 1519." Ulrich Zwingli: Zum Gedächtnis der Zürcher Reformation 1519-1919. Zurich: Berichthaus, 1919.

709. _____. "Zwingli im Jahre 1531." ZWA, 3, 1, 1913, 27.

64

710. Kobelt, Eduard. Die Bedeutung der Eidgenossenschaft
      für Huldrych Zwingli. Mitteilungen der antiquar-
      ischen Gesellschaft in Zürich, XLV. Zurich:
      Leeman A. G. 1970. [Zurich dissertation]

711. Kohler, Charles. Les Suisses dans les guerres
      à Italie de 1506 à 1512. Memoires et documents à
      publiés par la société d'histoire et d'archéo-
      logie de Genève. Vol. II. Geneva, 1896.

712. Köhler, Ludwig. "Eine Anspielung Zwinglis auf
      Erasmus." ZWA, 1, 14, 1903, 361-363.

713. _____. "Reformationsgedanken." Kirchenblatt
      für die reformierte Schweiz, 1918, pp. 205 ff.

714. _____. "Zwingli." NZZ, 1931. Nr. 1918.

715. Köhler, W. "Anmerkung zum Artikel: Zur
      Reformationsgeschichte Graubündens." ZWA, 4, 2,
      1921, 56.

716. _____. "Antistes Zwingli." ZWA, 3, 6, 1915, 194.

#717. _____. Armenpflege und Wohltätigkeit in Zürich zur
      Zeit Zwinglis. Neujahrsblatt der Hülfsgesell-
      schaft in Zürich, CXIX. Zurich: Schulthess,
      1919.
         R: E. Stauber, NZZ, 1919. Nr. 5.

718. _____. "Der Augsburger Reichstag von 1530 und
      die Schweiz." ZSKG, 3, 169-189.

719. _____. "Aus der Geschichte eines Zwinglibriefes."
      ZWA, 2, 4, 1914, 124-127.

720. _____. "Aus der Werkstatt der Zwingliausgabe."
      NZZ, 1938. Nr. 2145.

#721. _____. "Aus Zwinglis Bibliothek." ZKG, N.F. 3,
      1922, 41-73; N.F. 5, 1923, 49-76; N.F. 8,
      1926/27, 243-276.

722. _____. "Biographische Notizen zu den Bildern
      und Briefen." Ulrich Zwingli. Zum Gedächtnis
      der Zürcher Reformation, 1519-1919. Zurich:
      Berichthaus, 1919. Cols. 265-308.

#723. Köhler, Walther. <u>Das Buch der Reformation Huldrych</u>
<u>Zwinglis von ihm selbst und gleichzeitigen</u>
<u>Quellen erzählt</u>. Munich: E. Reinhardt, 1926, 1931.
R: L. von Muralt, ThL, 1931. Nr. 20;L.von Muralt,
ZWA, 4, 11, 1926, 346-347; K. Zimmermann,
ZWA, 4, 13, 1927, 409-410.

724. _____. "Eichhörnchen und Igel bei Zwingli."
<u>Theol. Blätter</u>, 8, 1929, 213-214.

725. _____. "Einführung in die Handschriftenproben
aus Zwingli. Briefwechsel." <u>Ulrich Zwingli</u>
<u>Zum Gedächtnis der Zürcher Reformation 1519-1919</u>.
Zurich: Berichthaus, 1919. 259-266.

726. _____. "Das Erbe Zwinglis in der Gegenwart."
ZWA, 3, 1916, 222.

727. _____. "Die erste Zürcher Disputation."
NZZ, 1923. Nr. 125.

728. _____. "Die Fernwirkungen Zwinglis." NZZ, 1931.
Nr. 1918.

#729. _____. <u>Die Geisteswelt Ulrich Zwinglis</u>.
<u>Christentum und Antike</u>. Gotha: Perthes, 1920.

730. _____. "Ein gunstiges Urteil Luthers über <u>Zwingli</u>?"
ZWA, 4, 5, 1923, 152-153.

731. _____. "Hessen und die Schweiz nach Zwinglis
Tode im Spiegel gleichzeitiger Korrespondenzen."
<u>Philipp der Grossmütige</u>. <u>Festschrift des</u>
<u>Hist. Vereins für das Grossherzogtum Hessen</u>.
Marburg: Elwert, 1904. 460-503.

732. _____. "Ein hessischer Pfarrer über Zwingli in
Marburg." ZWA, 2, 11, 1910, 321-325.

#733. _____. <u>Huldreich Zwingli</u>. Die Schweiz im
deutschen Geistesleben, IX. Leipzig: Haessel,
1923.
R: H. Escher, ZWA, 4, 6, 1923, 192;
H. Trog, NZZ, 1923. Nr. 1037.

#734. _____. <u>Huldrych Zwingli</u>. Leipzig: Koehler
& Amelang, 1943. 2nd ed., 1952.
R: Karl Barth, NZZ, 1944. Nr. 902;
Oskar Vasella, ZSKG, 39, 1945, 161-81

66

#735. Köhler, Walther. Huldrych Zwinglis Bibliothek.
Neujahrsblatt zum Besten des Waisenhauses,
LXXXIV. Zurich: Beer, 1921.
R: Ernst Staehlin, ZKG, 42, 1923, 443-444.

736. _____. "Huldrych Zwingli und das Reich."
Die Welt als Geschichte, 6, 1940, 1-14.

737. _____. "Ist das Zürcher Ratsmandat evangelischer
Predigt von 1520 ein angebliches?" ZWA, 2,
7, 1908, 208-214.

738. _____. "Jodocus Hesch." ZWA, 3, 8, 1916,
245-258.

739. _____. "Der Katzenelnbogische Erbfolgestreit im
Rahmen der allgemeinen Reformationsgeschichte
bis zum Jahre 1530." Mitteilungen des Oberhess.
Geschichtsvereins, 11, 1902, 1-30.

740. _____. "Kleine Beiträge zur Reformationsgeschichte.
1. Das sogenannte Bildnis Zwinglis in den
Uffizien." ZWA, 3, 11, 1918, 347-348.

741. _____. "Kleine Beiträge zur Reformations-
geschichte. Aus Zwinglis Bibliothek -- Zu
Zwinglis Schriften gegen Hieronymus Emser --
Eine Notiz zu Zwinglis Schwester."
ZWA, 4, 2, 1921, 60-63.

742. _____. "Luther und Zwingli." Zeitschrift für
Theologie und Kirche. N.F. 5, 1925.

#743. _____. Das Marburger Religionsgespräch 1529.
Versuch einer Rekonstruktion. Schriften des
Vereins für Reformationsgeschichte, CXLVIII.
Leipzig: Heinsius, 1929.
R: L. von Muralt, ZWA, 4, 3, 1930, 132-133.

744. _____. "Medizinisches bei Zwingli." Viertel-
jahrschrift der Naturforschenden Gesellschaft
in Zürich, 82, 1937, pp. 437 ff.

745. _____. "Ein modernes Glasgemälde mit dem
Bilde Zwinglis." ZWA, 3, 9, 1917, 285.

746. _____. "Nachklänge zur Zwinglifeier." Basler
Nachrichten, 1932. Nr. 22.

67

747. Köhler, Walther. "Nachtrag zu: Die 'göttliche Mühle' von E. Egli." ZWA, 2, 1910, 366-370.

748. _____. "Ein neuentdeckter Zwinglibrief." NZZ, 1925. Nr. 1564.

749. _____. "Die neuere Zwingli-Forschung." Theologische Rundschau, N.F. 4, 1932, 329-369.

750. _____. "Ein Plagiat an Zwingli." Vierteljahrsschrift der Naturforschenden Gesellschaft in Zürich, 82, 1937.

751. _____. "Die Post von Hessen nach der Schweiz zur Zeit Zwinglis und Bullingers." ZWA, 2, 6, 1907, 172-180.

#752. _____. "Die Randglossen Zwinglis zum Römerbrief." Forschungen zur Kirchengeschichte und zur Christlichen Kunst. Leipzig: Dieterich, 1931. 86-106.

#753. _____. "Das Religionsgespräch zu Marburg." ZWA, 5, 3, 1930, 81-102.

#754. _____. Das Religionsgespräch zu Marburg, 1529. Sammlung gemeinverständl. Vorträge und Schriften aus dem Gebiete der Theologie und Religionsgeschichte, CXL. Tübingen: Mohr, 1929.

755. _____. "Die Schweizer Taktik gegen Luther im Sakramentsstreit." ZWA, 2, 12, 1910, 356-362.

756. _____. "Eine schweizerische Reformationsgeschichte." ZWA, 2, 10, 1909, 317-318.

757. _____. "Ulrich Zwingli." NZZ, 1919. Nrs. 477, 483.

758. _____. "Ulrich Zwingli." Unsere religiösen Erzieher. Vol. II. 2nd ed. Leipzig: Quelle & Meyer, 1918. 45-77.

759. _____. "Ulrich Zwingli." Internat. Monatsschrift für Wissenschaft, Kunst und Technik, 13, 1919.

760. _____. "Ulrich Zwingli und der Krieg." Christliche Welt, 29, 1915, 675-682.

#761. Köhler, Walther. "Ulrich Zwingli und die Reformation in der Schweiz." Im Morgenrot der Reformation. Edited by Julius von Pflug-Harttung and S. Hersfeld. 3rd ed. Basel: Rodde, 1921.
    R: G. Meyer von Knonau, ZWA, 3, 1913, 27-28.

#762. _____. Ulrich Zwingli und die Reformation in der Schweiz. Religionsgeschichtliche Volksbücher für die deutsche christliche Gegenwart, IV. Tübingen: J. C. B. Mohr, 1919.
    R: G. Meyer von Knonau, ZWA, 2, 8, 1908, 243-245.

763. _____. "Ulrich Zwingli und seine Bedeutung für die Gegenwart." Christliche Welt, 27, 1913, 314-318, 338-346.

764. _____. "Um des Glaubens willen." Sonntagsblatt der Basler Nachrichten, 1931. Nr. 41.

765. _____. "Ein Urteil Friedrichs des Grossen über Zwingli." ZWA, 2, 16, 1912, 508-510.

766. _____. "Usteri, Johann Martin: Initia Zwingli. Beiträge zur Geschichte der Studien und der Geistesentwicklung Zwinglis in der Zeit vor Beginn der Reformation. Theolog. Studien und Kritiken. 58, 1885." Theologische Rundschau, N.F. 4, 1932.

767. _____. "Der Verfasser des 'Libellus confutationis' in Zwinglis 'In catabaptistarum strophas elenchus.'" Mennonitische Geschichtsblätter, 3, 1938.

768. _____. "Warum sind Luther und Zwingli 1529 in Marburg nicht einig geworden?" Nederlandsch Archief voor Kerkgeschiedenis. N.S. 22, 1929.

769. _____. "Weitere Beiträge zur Geschichte des Titels 'Antistes'." ZWA, 3, 11, 1918, 350-351.

770. _____. "Wirkung Zwinglis auf das niederländische Luthertum." ZWA, 3, 9, 1917, 268-270.

69

771. Köhler, Walther. "Wirkungen Zwinglis und Bullingers
     auf das Ausland," ZWA, 3, 1, 1913, 24-27.

772. _____. "Würdigung des Entschuldigungsbriefes
     Zwinglis an Heinrich Utinger vom 5. Dezember
     1518." ZWA, 2, 4, 1914, 128.

773. _____. "Zu Antistes Zwingli." ZWA, 3, 9,
     1917, 284-285.

774. _____. "Zu einem Gedicht gegen Zwingli."
     ZWA, 1, 1913.

775. _____. "Zu Luther und Zwingli." ZWA, 3, 10,
     1917, 321-322.

776. _____. "Zu: Zwingli und Luther." ZWA, 3, 9, 1916,
     270-273.

777. _____. "Zu Zwingli und Pindar." ZWA, 5, 2,
     1929, 71-72.

778. _____. "Zu Zwinglis Abreise nach Marburg, 1529."
     ZWA, 3, 7, 1916, 222-223.

779. _____. "Zu Zwinglis ältester Abendmahlsauf-
     fassung." ZKG, 45, 1926/1927, 399-408.

780. _____. "Zu Zwinglis (angeblichem?) Pariser
     Studienaufenthalt." ZWA, 4, 2, 1921, 46-51.

781. _____. "Zu Zwinglis französischen Bündnisplänen."
     ZWA, 4, 10, 1925, 302-311.

782. _____. "Zum Abendmahlsstreite zwischen Luther
     und Zwingli." Lutherstudien. Zur 4 Jahrhundertfeier
     der Reformation veröffentlicht von den Mit-
     arbeitern der Weimarer Lutherausgabe. Weimar:
     Böhlau, 1917. 114-139.

783. _____. "Zum Gedächtnis der ersten evangelischen
     Abendmahlsfeier in Zürich." NZZ, 1925. Nr. 531.

784. _____. "Zum Religions Gespräch von Marburg
     1529." Festgabe für Gerold Meyer von Knonau.
     Zurich: Berichthaus, 1913. 359-381.

785. Köhler, Walther. "Zur Abendmahls Kontroverse in
der Reformationszeit insbesondere zur
Entwicklung der Abendmahlslehre Zwinglis."
ZKG, 47, 1928, 47-56.

786. _____. "Zur Geschichte der Pfarrbücher."
ZWA, 3, 16, 1920, 527-528.

787. _____. "Zur Geschichte der privaten Abendmahls-
feier." ZWA, 3, 2, 1913, 58-64.

788. _____. Zürcher Ehegericht und Genfer Konsistorium.
I: Das Zürcher Ehegericht und seine Auswirkungen
in der deutschen Schweiz zur Zeit Zwinglis.
Quellen und Abhandlungen zur schweizerischen
Reformationsgeschichte, N.F. VII. Leipzig:
Hensius, 1932.
    R: Hermann Escher, ZWA, 5, 9, 1933, 413;
    ZWA, 5, 10, 1933, 455-458.

789. _____. "Die zweite Zürcher Disputation, 26.-28.
Okt. 1523." NZZ, 1923. Nr. 1477.

790. _____. "Zwingli als päpstlicher Akolouthenkaplan."
ZWA, 3, 5, 1915, 154.

#791. _____. "Zwingli als Theologe." Ulrich Zwingli:
Zum Gedächtnis der Zürcher Reformator 1519-1919.
Zurich: Berichthaus, 1919. 9-74.

792. _____. "Ein Zwingli-Autograph aus dem Kestner
Museum in Hannover." ZWA, 4, 2, 1921, 56-58.

793. _____. "Zwingli, Huldrych." Calwer Kirchenle-
xikon 2, 1941.

794. _____. "Zwingli, Huldreich, 1484-1531."
Encyclopaedia of the Social Sciences, 15, 1935,
542-543.

795. _____. "Zwingli in Köln." NZZ, 1934. Nr. 212.

796. _____. "Zwingli Student in Paris?" ZWA 3,
12/13, 1918/1919, 414-417.

797. _____. "Zwingli. Ulrich, besser Huldrych."
Die Religion in Geschichte und Gegenwart, 2nd Edition. 5,
2152-2158.

798. Köhler, Walther. "Zwingli und Basel," ZWA, 5, 1, 1929, 2-10.

799. _____. "Zwingli und Bern." Forschungen und Fortschritte, 4, 1928, 231-232.

#800. _____. Zwingli und Bern. Sammlung gemeinverständlicher Vorträge und Schriften aus dem Gebiete der Theologie und Religionsgeschichte, CXXXII. Tübingen: J. C. B. Mohr, 1928.

801. _____. "Zwingli und Italien." Aus fünf Jahrhunderten schweizerischer Kirchengeschichte. Basel: Helbing, 1932. 22-38.
    R: NZZ, 1932. Nr. 797.

#802. _____. Zwingli und Luther. Ihr Streit über das Abendmahl nach seinen politischen und religiösen Beziehungen. 2 vols. Quellen und Forschungen zur Reformations-Geschichte, VI, VII. Vol. I: Leipzig, 1924. Vol. II: Gütersloh, 1953.
    R: R. Pfister, Archiv, 47, 1956, 132-134;
    H. Escher, ZWA, 4, 8, 1924, 249-255;
    E. Bizer, ZKG, 70, 3/4, 1959, 335-337.

803. _____. "Zwingli und die Murmeltiere." Theologische Blätter, 5, 1926, 290-291.

804. _____. "Zwingli und Schleiermacher." ZWA, 4, 3, 1922, 92-93.

805. _____. "Zwingli und Strassburg." Elsass-Lothringisches Jahrbuch, 20, 1942, 145-180.

806. _____. "Zwingli vor Ehegericht." Festgabe des Zwinglivereins zum 70. Geburtstag seines Präsidenten Hermann Escher. Zurich: Zwingliverein, 1927. 166-211.

807. _____. "Zwingliana in Wildhaus und Einsiedeln." ZWA, 6, 1, 1934, 1-4.

808. _____. "Zwinglis Beziehungen zu Bern." ZWA, 4, 15, 1928, 450-455.

809. _____. "Zwinglis Glaubensbekenntnis." ZWA, 1931, 242-261.

810. Köhler, Walther, "Zwinglis letzte Predigten."
ZWA, 2, 16, 1912, 506-508.

811. _____. "Zwinglis Lieblingsspruch." NZZ,
1931. Nr. 1982.

812. _____. "Zwinglis Lied." ZWA, 2, 14, 1911,
439-441.

#813. _____. "Zwinglis religiöse Eigenart."
Schweizerische Akademiereden. Edited by
Fritz Strich. Bern, 1945. 297-312. See also:
Die Schweiz, Illustrierte Zeitschrift, 23, 1919,
pp. 3 ff.

#814. Köhler, Walther, Farner, Oskar; Oechsli, Wilhelm;
et al. Ulrich Zwingli 1519-1919. Zum Gedächtnis
der Zürcher Reformation. Zurich, Berichthaus,
1919.

815. Kok, W. M. "Ulrich Zwingli." Gereformeerd theolog.
Tijdschr., 1931. Nr. 6.

816. Kollbrunner, U. "Zwingli und die Schule." Der
Protestant, 1918. Nr. 26.

817. König, Th. Ulrich Zwingli. 3 vols. Leipzig,
1862. [*]

818. Krause, G. "Zwinglis Auslegung der Propheten."
ZWA, 11, 1960, 257-265.

819. Kreienbühler, Johann. Zwingli und das Messopfer.
Zurich: A. Müller, 1927.

820. Kressner, H. "Schweizer Ursprünge des anglikanischen
Staatskirchentums." Schriften des Vereins
für Reformationsgeschichte, 59, 1953, 170.
R: J. H. S. Burleigh, SJT, 8, 1955,
209-211.

821. Kreutzer, Jakob. Zwinglis Lehre von der Obrigkeit.
Kirchenrechtliche Abhandlungen, LVII.
Stuttgart: Union Deutsche Verlagsgesellschaft,
1909. Reprint: Amsterdam, 1965.

822. Krönert, Georg. "Luther und Zwingli. Ein Beitrag
zur evangel. Irenik." Die Reformierte Schweiz,
1954, 3, 78-80.

823. Krönler, Hans. Der Kult der Eucharistie in
      Sprache und Volkstum der deutschen Schweiz.
      Schriften der Schweizer. Gesellschaft für
      Volkskunde, XXXIII. Basel, 1949. [Freiburg
      dissertation]

824. Kubly-Müller, Joh. Jakob. "Die Reformator
      Zwingli-Familie in Verbindung mit Glarus."
      Neue Glarner Zeitung, 1919. Nr. 647.

#825. Kügelgen, Constantin von. Die Ethik Huldrych
      Zwinglis. Leipzig: R. Wopke, 1902.
          R: J. I. Good, Princeton Theological
      Review, 4, 1906, 276; P. Christ, ZWA, 1,
      12, 1902, 319-320.

826. _____. Zwinglis Vademekum für gebildete
      Jünglinge. Zeitgemässe Traktate aus der
      Reformationszeit, IV. Leipzig: Richard
      Wöpke, 1904.

827. Kuhn, Georg. "Zwingli und Luther." Glarner
      Nachrichten, 1931. Nr. 236.

828. Kunz, K. "Hat Zwingli die ältesten Pfarrbücher
      eingeführt?" ZSKG, 14, 1920.

829. Künzli, Edwin. "Antwort an Paul Marti von
      Edwin Künzli." ZWA, 9, 6, 1951, 375-377.

830. _____. "Der Mann bei Zwingli." ZWA, 11, 6,
      1961, 351-371.

831. _____. "Der Prediger Huldrych Zwingli."
      NZZ, 1969. Nr. 4.

832. _____. "Quellenproblem und mystischer Schriftsinn
      in Zwinglis Genesis- und Exodus-Kommentar."
      ZWA, 9, 4, 1950, 185-207. Also: ZWA, 9, 5,
      1951, 253-307.
          R: Paul Marti, ZWA, 9, 6, 1951, 365-374.

#833. _____. "Zwingli als Ausleger des Alten Testaments."
      Zwinglis sämtliche Werke, 14, pp. 871 ff.

834. _____. Zwingli als Ausleger von Genesis und
      Exodus. Zurich: Berichthaus, 1950. [Zurich
      dissertation]

835. Kunzli, Edwin. "Zwinglis Jesaja-Erklärungen."
ZWA, 10, 8, 1957, 488-491.

836. _____. "Zwinglis Stellung zu den Juden."
Festgabe Leonhard von Muralt. Edited by
Martin Haas and Rene Hauswirth. Zurich:
Berichthaus, 1970. 309-318.

837. Lang, August. "Die Augsburger Bekenntnisse
Zwinglis und Butzers." Reformierte Kirchenzeitung,
Wupperthal, 1930. Nr. 32; Kirchenzeitung der
reformierte Kirche in den U.S.A., 1930. Nr. 41.

838. _____. "Ulrich Zwingli." Reformierte Kirchenzeitung, Wupperthal, 82, 321.

839. _____. "Ulrich Zwingli; ein Gedenkwort zu
sein 400. Sterbetage." Das Evangel. Deutschland;
Kirchl. Rundschau des Deutsch. Evang. Kirchen-
bundes. 1931. Nrs. 41, 42.

840. _____. "Ulrich Zwingli; zu sein 400. Sterbetage,
11. Okt. 1931." Kirchenzeitung der Reformierte
Kirche in den U.S.A., 1931. Nr. 38. See also:
Reformierte Kirchenzeitung, Wupperthal, 1931.
Nr. 41.

#841. _____. Zwingli und Calvin. Monographien zur
Weltgeshichte, XXXI. Bielefeld & Leipzig:
Volhagen & Klasing, 1913.
R: W. Köhler, ZWA, 3, 3, 1914, 90-91;
W. Köhler, Theologische Rundschau, N.F. 4, 1932;
Bess, ZKG, 35, 1914, 133-134; F. W. Loetscher,
4, 1906, 325-326; Ch. Schnetzler, Revue,
N.S. 1, 1913, 384-391.

842. Lang, Theodor. "Zwingli." Evangel. Bund zur
Wahrung der deutsch-protest. Interessen, 45,
1931, 5.

843. _____. "Zwingli; z. 400jähr. Todestag 1531.
11. Okt. 1931." Die Wartburg, 1931. Nr. 9.

#844. Largiadèr, Anton. Geschichte von Stadt und
Landschaft Zürich. Vol. I: Von den Anfängen
bis zur Aufklärung. Erlenbach-Zurich: Rentsch, 1945

75

845. Largiadèr, Anton. "Die Kappeler Milchsuppe."
NZZ, 1931. Nr. 1885.

846. _____. "Das reformierte Zürich und die Fest-
und Heiligentage." ZWA, 9, 9, 1953, 497-525.

847. _____. "Die Sammlung der Zwingli-Schriften
im Staatsarchiv Zürich." ZWA, 10, 9, 1958,
573-579.

848. _____. Untersuchungen zur zürcherischen Landes-
hoheit. Zurich: Schulthess & co., 1920.
R: W. Köhler, ZWA, 4, 1, 1921, 28-29.

849. _____. "Zur Geschichte des zweiten Kappelerkrieges." ZWA, 6, 8, 1937, 460-462.

850. "Lateinisches Gedicht des Gerardus Noviomagus
auf Zwinglis Tod." ZWA, 2, 12, 1910, 362-
363.

851. Lauterburg, Peter. "Die Informationstätigkeit
der zürichfreundlichen Berner. (Zwei Beispiele
aus dem Jahr 1531)." ZWA, 12, 3, 1965,
207-221.

852. L'Ebraly, Charles. La doctrine sacramentaire de
Ulrich Zwingli. Paris: Beauchesne, 1939.

853. Lechner, Ad. "Zwinglis Hütte." ZWA, 2, 8, 1908,
246-247. [*]

854. Leemann, Paul van Elck. "An der Wiege der
Zwinglibibel." NZZ, 1942. Nr. 1021.

855. Lehmann, H. "Erinnerungen an Ulrich Zwingli."
ZWA, 2, 13, 1911, 387-391.

856. _____. "Zwingli und die zürcherische Kunst im
Zeitalter der Reformation." Ulrich Zwingli:
Zum Gedächtnis der Zürcher Reformation 1519-1919.
Zurich: Berichthaus, 1919.

857. Lehmann, Max. "Luther und Zwingli." Preussische
Jahrbucher, 163, 1916, 13-25.

858. Lemaître, Auguste. Calvin et Luther. Geneva, 1959.

859.   Lenz, Max. "Zwingli und Landgraf Philipp,"
       Zeitschrift für Kirchengeschichte, 3, 1879. 28-62.

860.   Lerch, David. "Zur Beziehung zwischen Zwinglis
       und Johannes Wilds Genesisauslegung." Theologische
       Zeitschrift, 8, 1952, 471-472.

#861. Ley, Roger. Kirchenzucht bei Zwingli. Quellen
       und Abhandlungen zur Geschichte des Schweizerischen
       Protestantismus, II. Zurich: Zwingli Verlag,
       1948. [Zurich dissertation]

862.   Lichtenhahn, Fritz. "Das protestantische Ja und
       Nein." Protestant, 34. Nr. 20.

863.   _____. "Zwinglis häusliches Leben." Protestant,
       1918. Nr. 24.

864.   Liebenau, Th. von. Gilg Tschudis Beschreibung
       des Kappelerkrieges. Archiv für schweizerische
       Reformationsgeschichte, I.

865.   Liermann, H. "Untersuchungen zum Sakralrecht
       des protestantischen Herrschers." Zeitschrift
       d. Savigny-Stiftung Kanon, 1941. Nr. 30.

866.   Lindsay, T. M. "The Reformation in Switzerland under
       Zwingli." A History of the Reformation. Vol. II.
       Edinburgh: Clark, 1907. 21-60.
         R: W. Köhler, Theologische Rundschau, 15. 1912.

867.   Linn, Charles Adolphus. Butzer and the Eucharistic
       Controversy between Luther and Zwingli. Hartford,
       1924. [Hartford S.T.M. thesis]

868.   Lippert, J. "Die Einladung Zwinglis an Johann
       Eck zum Berner Religionsgespräch." ZWA, 10,
       1938, 580-588.

869.   Locher, Gottfried W. "Eine alte Deutung des
       Namens Zwingli." ZWA, 9, 5, 1951, 307-310.

#870. _____. "The Change in the understanding of
       Zwingli in Recent Research." JCH, 34, 1,
       March 1965, 3-24.

871.   _____. "'Christus unser Hauptmann', ein
       Stück der Verkündigung Huldrych Zwinglis."
       ZWA, 9, 3, 1950, 121-138.See. Nr. 879

872. Locher, Gottfried W. Der Eigentumsbegriff als
      Problem evangelischer Theologie. Studien
      z. Dogmengeschichte und systematischen Theologie,
      V. Zurich: Zwingli Verlag, 1954.
         R: Karl Fueter, NZZ, 1955. Nr. 1057.

873. _____. Die evangelische Stellung der Reformatoren
      zum öffentlichen Leben. Kirchliche Zeitfragen,
      XXVI. Zurich: Zwingli Verlag, 1950.

874. _____. "Elia bei Zwingli." Judaica, 9, 1,
      1953, 62-63.

875. _____. "Geist und Gemeinschaft -- Theologie
      in öffentlicher Verantwortung. Zur 450-Jahr-
      Feier der Reformation Huldrych Zwinglis."
      Reformierte Kirchenzeitung, 1969, 1, 79.
      See also: Kirchenblatt für die reformierte
      Schweiz, 1969, 3, 34-36.

876. _____. "Das Geschichtsbild Huldrych Zwinglis."
      Theologische Zeitschrift, 9, 1953, 275-302.
      See also: NZZ, 1953. Nr. 523. See: Nr. 879.

#877. _____. "Grundzüge der Theologie Huldrych
      Zwinglis im Vergleich mit derjenigen Martin
      Luthers und Johannes Calvins. Ein Überblick."
      ZWA, 12, 7, 1967, 470-509; ZWA, 12, 8, 1967,
      545-595. See: Nr. 879.

#878. _____. Grundzüge der Theologie Huldrych Zwinglis
      im Vergleich mit derjenigen Martin Luthers und
      Johannes Calvins. Zurich: Berichthaus, 1968.

#879. _____. Huldrych Zwingli in neuer Sicht, Zehn
      Beiträge zur Theologie der Zürcher Reformation.
      Zurich, Stuttgart: Zwingli Verlag, 1969.
         R: Lewis Spitz, Sr. Concordia Theological
      Monthly, 41, 1970, 2, 121-122; L. von
      Muralt, ZWA, 13, 2, 1969, 147-148; F. Büsser,
      NZZ,1969.Nr. 436.

880. _____. "Huldrych Zwinglis Botschaft." ZWA, 10,
      10, 1958, 591-602. See Nr.879

881. _____. Im Geist und in der Wahrheit: die
      reformatorische Wendung im Gottesdienst zu Zürich.
      Neukirchen: Verlag der Buchhandlung des Erziehungs-
      vereins, 1957. See Nr.879
         R: A.Eichenberger, ZSKG, 52, 1958, 275-276.

882. Locher, Gottfried W. "Inhalt und Absicht von
      Zwinglis Marienlehre." Kirchenblatt für die
      reformierte Schweiz, 107, 1951, 3, 34-37.
      See also: NZZ, 1951. Nrs. 8, 13. See: Nr. 879.
        R: L. von Muralt, ZWA, 9, 8, 1952, 490.

883. _____. "Die Legende vom Herzen Zwinglis neu
      untersucht." ZWA, 9, 10, 1953, 563-576.

#884. _____. "Die Prädestinationslehre Huldrych
      Zwinglis." Theologische Zeitschrift, 12,
      September/October 1956, 526-548. See: Nr. 879.

885. _____. "The Shape of Zwingli's Theology. A
      Comparison with Luther and Calvin." Translated
      by J. A. Morrison, revised by J. Adams.
      Pittsburgh Perspective, 8, 2, 1967, 5-26.

#886. _____. Die Theologie Huldrych Zwinglis im Lichte
      seiner Christologie. Vol. I: Die Gotteslehre.
      Studien z. Dogmengesch. und systematische
      Theologie, I. Zurich: Zwingli Verlag, 1952.
      [Zurich dissertation]
        R: Fritz Blanke, Kirchenblatt für die
      reformierte Schweiz, 1952, 129-131;
      P. Scherding. RHPR, 35, 4, 1955, 503-505;
      F. Schmidt-Clausing, ThL, 79, 1954, 313-314;
      P. Gander, Revue de Theologie et de Philosophie,
      3, 1953, 211-212; P. Burckhardt, ThZ, 9,
      1953, 460-462. R. Pfister, ZWA, 9,8,1952,445-452.

#887. _____. "Die theologische und politische Bedeutung
      des Abendmahlsstreites im Licht von Zwinglis
      Briefen." ZWA, 13, 5, 1971, 281-304.

#888. _____. "Wandlungen des Zwingli-Bildes."
      Vox theologica; interacademiaal theologisch
      tijdschrift, 32, 6, 1962, 169-186. See: Nr. 879.

889. _____. "Zu Zwinglis 'Professio fidei'.
      Beobachtungen und Erwägungen zur Pariser
      Reinschrift der sogennanter Fidei Expositio."
      ZWA, 12, 10, 1968, 689-700.

890. _____. "Zwingli, II. Theologie." Die Religion
      in Geschichte und Gegenwart, 3rd Edition 6, 1969,
      1960-1969.

#891. Locher, Gottfried W. "Zwingli und Erasmus."
       ZWA, 13, 1, 1969, 37-61. See also:
       Scrinium Erasmianum, 2, 1970. Also: Kirchen-
       blatt für die reformierte Schweiz, 1969,
       15/16, 225-29, 242-246.

892. Löhr, Josef. "Methodisch-Kritische Beiträge zur
      Geschichte der Sittlichkeit des Klerus."
      Reformationsgeschichtliche Studien und Texte,
      17, 1910.

893. Lunzen, H. van. "Hoe Zwitserland zijn grooten
      Hervormer eert." Ons godsdienstig Leven,
      Hoorn, 1931. Nr. 40.

894. _____. "Waarom wij Zwingli herdenken." Ons
      godsdienstig Leven, Hoorn, 1931. Nr. 40.

895. _____. "Zwingli-Bibliographie." Ons godsdienstig
      Leven, Hoorn, 1931. Nr. 40.

896. Lüscher, Arnold. "Zwingli und die kommende
      Zeit." Schweizerische Lehrerzeitung, 76. Nr. 41.

897. "Luther und Zwingli." Der Protestant. 1918.
      Nr. 41.

898. "Luther und Zwingli, oder freimütige und wohl-
      gemeinte Gedanken über die Trennung und
      Wiedervereinigung der Lutheraner und
      Reformierten. Für den Bürger und Landmann."
      Meiningen, 1918.

899. Maag, Albert. "Von einem Brief Zwinglis an den
      Rat zu Biel." ZWA, 2, 5, 1907, 154-155.

900. Maire, Marguerite. "Une belle figure de
      notre histoire: Le réformateur Ulrich
      Zwingli." Messager social [de l'Église
      protest., Genève], 1931. Nr. 14.

901. Manning, D. Wilson. The Relation of Zwingli to
      the Swiss Anabaptists. Waco, Texas, 1952.
      [Master of Arts thesis, Baylor University]

902. Mannsdorfer, Hans. Huldreich Zwingli, der
      Staatsmann. Zurich: Verlag Volk und Schrifttum,
      1941.

903. Mantel, Alfred. "Nach der Schlacht bei Kappel."
Zürichsee-Zeitung, 1931. Nr. 294, 296; Anzeiger
von Uster, 1931. Nr. 236.

904. Maron, F. "Ulrich Zwingli und unsere Zeit."
Aroser Zeitung, 1931. Nr. 4.

905. Marti, Paul. "Charakter und Schichksal bei
Zwingli." Schweizerische reformierte Volksblatt,
1931. Nr. 4.

906. _____. "Mystischer Schriftsinn und wissenschaft-
liche Auslegung des Alten Testaments." ZWA,
9, 6, 1951, 365-375.

907. Matthes, Otto. "Zwingli; z. 400. Todestag."
Die Volkskirche; evang. Monatsblatt für
Württemberg, 1931. Nr. 10/11.

908. Maurer, Adolf. "Am Zwinglistein bei Kappel."
Evangelischer Kirchenbote für den Kanton
Thurgau, 1931. Nr. 10. [*]

909. _____. "Der Balz." Der Zwinglikalender, 1930,
24-25. [*]

910. _____. "Der Bettler vom St. Peter." Der
Zwinglikalender, 1920, 21. See also: Auf
der Wanderschaft, Gedichte, 58-60. [*]

911. _____. "Doet in Gods naam een dappere daad
in uw lewen." Ons godsdienstig Leven, Hoorn,
1931. Nr. 40.

912. _____. "Du hast um Gott gerungen (Am Zwinglistein)."
Der Zwinglikalender, 1931. 16.

913. _____. Huldrych Zwingli; z. Gedächtnis seines
Todes bei Kappel a. A. am 11. Okt. 1531. Zurich:
Fehr-Tschudi, 1931.

914. _____. "Der Manz. Erzählung aus dem Leben
Zwinglis." Der Zwinglikalender, 1919, 21-23.

915. _____. "Die Manzin. Erzählung aus Zwinglis Zeit."
Der Zwinglikalender, 1920. 22-28.

81

916. Maurer, Adolf. "Die Schlacht bei Kappel."
      Thurgauer Zeitung, 1931. Nr. 238.

917. _____. "Ulrich Zwingli und unsere heutige
      Zeit." St. Galler Tagblatt, 1931. Nr. 476.

918. _____. "Eine Wolke von Zeugen." Kirchenbote
      für den Kanton Zurich, 1933. Nr. 1.

919. _____. "Zwingli." Der Zwingli Kalender, 1919,
      17.

920. _____. "Zwingli." Kirchenbote für den Kanton
      Zürich, 1931. Nr. 10; Evangel. Gemeindeblatt,
      1931, Nr. 10. [*]

921. _____. "Zwingli und sein Organist." Der Zwingli
      Kalender, 1919, 31. See also: Auf der
      Wanderschaft, Gedichte, 43. [*]

922. _____. "Zwinglilied." Der Zwingli Kalender,
      1919, 19. See also: Auf der Wanderschaft,
      Gedichte, 42. [*]

923. Maxwell, William D. An Outline of Christian Worship.
      London: Oxford University Press, 1940.

924. McBride, Jerold Robert. "Authority and Interpre-
      tation in Zwingli and Melanchthon." Fort Worth,
      Texas: Southwestern Baptist Theological Seminary
      Library, 1957.

925. McGiffert, Arthur C. "Huldreich Zwingli."
      Protestant Thought before Kant. New York, 1931

926. McLelland, J. C. "Covenant Theology: a re-
      evaluation." Candler Journal of Theology, 3,
      July 1957, 182-188.

#927. McNeill, John T. "Huldreich Zwingli and the Reformation
      in German Switzerland." History and Character of
      Calvinism. New York: Oxford University Press, 1962.

928. McShane, E. D. "Zwinglianism." New Catholic
      Encyclopedia. Vol. 14. New York: McGraw Hill
      Book Co., 1967. 1143-1144.

929. Mecenseffy, Grete. "Zwinglijubiläum in Zürich,"
      Reformiertes Kirchenblatt, 46, 1969, 1/6.

930. Meier, Adolf. "Zwinglis Übersetzung des Römer-
     briefes." Evangelische Theologie, 19,
     1959, 40-52.

931. Meier, P. Gabriel, O.S.B. Schweizerische
     Reformationsgeschichte. Geschichtlichen
     Jugend- und Volksbibliothek, XLVIII.
     Regensburg: Verlagsanstalt, 1916.
         R: G. M. von Knonau, ZWA, 3, 7, 1916, 223.

932. _____. "Ulrich Zwingli." Wetzer und Welte.
     Katholisches Kirchenlexikon. 2nd ed. Vol. 12.
     pp. 2024 ff.

933. Meister, Leonhard. Ulrich Zwingli, ein
     vaterländisches Schauspiel. Zurich, 1794. [*]

934. Meister, Willi. Volksbildung und Volkserziehung
     in der Reformation Huldrych Zwinglis. Erziehung
     und Schule, V. Zurich: Zwingli Verlag, 1939.
     [Zurich dissertation]

935. Meltzer, Hermann. "Das Nationale und Soziale
     bei Zwingli." Die Hilfe, 1931. Nr. 42/43.

936. _____. "Zum 400. Todestage Zwinglis."
     N. sächsisches Kirchenblatt, 1931. Nrs. 41, 42,
     44.

937. _____. "Zwingli im deutsch-evangelischen
     Religionsunterricht." Zeitschrift für den
     evangelischen Religionsunterricht, 42. Nrs. 5, 7.

938. _____. "Zwingli-Literatur." Zeitschrift für
     den evangelischen Religionsunterricht, 42, 1931,
     299-304.

939. _____. "Zwingli und Luther." Nordisches Sächsisches
     Kirchenblatt, 1933, 31-38.

940. Mercier, Charles. "Doctrines religieuses et
     doctrines politiques au XVIe Siècle: Zwingli"
     Revue de synthèse, 13, 1937, 17-26.

941. Mesnard, Pierre. "La pédagogie évangélique de
     Zwingli." Revue Thomiste, 53, 1953, 367-
     386.

942. Mettler, Art. "Zwingli und die Täufer."
      Kirchenblatt für die reformierte Schweiz, 115,
      1959, 66-68.

943. Meyer, C. F. "Festkantate zur Weihe des Zwingli-
      Denkmals (25. August 1885)." NZZ, 1885. Nr. 234.
      See also: Errinnerungsblätter zur Einweihung
      des Zwingli-Denkmals in Zürich, 1885, 2,
      pp. 30 ff. [*]

944. _____. "Lagerreligion." Huttens letzte Tage.3rd ed.
      Leipzig, 1881. 123. [*]

945. _____. "Der Rappe des Komturs." Das Schweizer-
      haus, ein vaterländisches Taschenbuch auf das
      Jahr 1874. Bern, 1873. 37. See also: Gedichte,
      Leipzig, 1882. 307. [*]

946. _____. "Redensarten." Huttens letzte Tage. 3rd ed.
      Leipzig, 1881. 78. [*]

947. _____. "Der Uli." Huttens letzte Tage. 3rd ed.
      Leipzig, 1881. 76. [*]

948. _____. "Zwingli (Ein Brief von Zwingli kommt)."
      Huttens letzte Tage. Leipzig, 1872. 55. [*]

949. Meyer, Ernst. "La mort d'Ulrich Zwingli."
      Semaine religieuse, 1931. Nr. 41.

950. _____. "Zwingli und die Kappelerkriege."
      Bund, 1931. Nr. 578.

951. Meyer, Helmut. Die Vorgeschichte des zweiten
      Kappelerkrieges. Zurich, 1968. [Zurich
      dissertation]

952. Meyer, Paul. "Bibel und Schwert; z. 400.
      Todestag des Reformators Ulr. Zwingli."
      Appenzeller Zeitung, 1931. Nr. 238.

#953. _____. Zwinglis Soziallehren. Linz a. d.
      Donau, Verlagsgesellschaft, 1921.
         R: W. Köhler, ZWA, 4, 2, 1921, 64;
         W. Köhler, ZKG, 44, 1925, 131-132.

954. Meyer, Wilhelm Josef. "Ein ungedrucktes Lied
      über Zwingli." ZWA, 2, 1911, 441-444.

955. Meyer, Wilhelm Josef. "Zwingli, Ulrich
       (Huldreich)." The Catholic Encyclopedia.
       Vol. 15. New York: The Gilmary Society,
       1940. 772-775.

956. Michel, Alfred. "Thomas Bornhauser; z. Todes-
       feier Zwinglis." Kirchenbote für den Kanton
       Thurgau, 1931. Nr. 10.

#956a. Moeller, Bernd. "Zwinglis Disputationen." Zeitschrift
       d. Savigny-Stiftung f. Rechtsgeschichte. Kanonistische
       Abt., 56, 1970, 275-324.

957. Moppert, Oscar. "Literatur zum Zwingli-
       Gedächtnis." Die Garbe, 15, 2.

958. _____. "Zwinglis Glaube." Die Garbe, 15, 1.

959. Morf, Hans. "Obrigkeit und Kirche in Zürich bis
       zu Beginn der Reformation." ZWA, 13, 3,
       1970, 164-205.

960. _____. "Zunftverfassung, Obrigkeit, und
       Kirche in Zürich von Waldmann bis Zwingli."
       Mitteilungen der antiquarischen Gesellschaft
       in Zürich, 45, 1, 1969.

961. Moser, Andreas. "Die Anfänge der Freundschaft
       zwischen Zwingli und Oecolampad." ZWA, 10,
       1958, 614-620.

962. _____. "Franz Lamberts Reise durch die Schweiz
       im Jahre 1522." ZWA, 10, 7, 1957, 467-471.

963. Mosse, George L. "Zwingli, Huldreich." The World
       Book Encyclopedia. Vol. 20. Chicago: Field
       Enterprises Educational Corporation, 1967. 510.

964. Moyer, Elgin S. "Zwingli, Ulrich (Huldreich)."
       Who was Who in Church History. Chicago:
       Moody Press, 1962. 452.

965. Mühlhausen, Rudolf. "Zwingli, dem Zürcher
       Reformator z. Gedächtnis." Illustrierte
       Zeitung, 1931. Nr. 4517.

966. Mulder, D. "Hans Abegg, tijdgenoot en uit
       beelder van Zwinglis leven." Ons godsdienstig
       Leven, Hoorn, 1931. Nr. 40.

967. Müller, Adolf. "Huldrych Zwingli und unsere heutige Zeit." Anzeiger von Uster, 1931. Nr. 236.

968. _____. "Zum 400. Todestag Ulrich Zwinglis." Berner Heim, 1931. Nr. 41. Supplement to Berner Tagblatt.

969. _____. "Zwingli als Führer in Vergangenheit und Gegenwart." Schweiz. Volksblatt von Bachtel, 1931. Nr. 156.

970. _____. "Zwingli als Führer zum Wort Gottes; z. 400. Todestag am 11. Okt. (1931)." Zofinger Tagblatt, 1931. Nr. 237; Rheintaler, 1931. Nr. 119; Schweiz. evangelisches Schulblatt, 1931. Nr. 41.

971. _____. "Zwinglis Tod." Rheintaler, 1931. Nr. 119.

972. Müller, Aloys. "Der Landfriede von Deinikon 16./20., Nov. 1531; eine Friedenswerk und seine rechtsgesch. Entwicklung." Baar, 1931

973. Müller, Erich Siegfried. "Huldreich Zwingli; zu s. Todestag." Grosse Ausgabe. Kaiserslautern, 1931.

974. _____. "Huldreich Zwinglis Abschied." Huldreich Zwingli. Kaiserslautern, 1931. 25-32. [*]

975. _____. Sonne über dem See. Leipzig, 1931. [*]

976. Müller, Ernst. Ulrich Zwingli. Berner Volksschriften, XII. Bern: Berner Volksschriften-Verlag.

977. Müller, G. E. "Zwingli as a religious philosopher." The Hibbert Journal, 58, 1960, 164-169.

978. Müller, Joseph Th. "Die Böhmische Brüderunität und Zwingli." ZWA, 3, 16, 1920, 514-524.

979. Muralt, Leonhard von. "Die Abgekürzte Bezeichnung der Zwingli-Ausgaben." ZWA, 10, 9, 1958, 582.

86

980. Muralt, Leonhard von. "Der Anfang der Reformation in Zürich." Reformatio, 18, January 1969, 3-9.

#981. _____. Die Badener Disputation 1526. Quellen und Abhandlungen zur schweizerischen Reformationsgeschichte, III. Leipzig, 1926. R: W. Köhler, NZZ, 1926. Nr. 119; W. Köhler, Theologische Rundschau, N.F. 4, 1932. M. Heinsius Nachfolger.

982. _____. "Der Durchbruch der Reformation in Zürich." Der Zwingli-Kalender 1934. Edited by a circle of Zurich pastors. Basel: Friedr. Reinhardt, 1934.

983. _____. "Der Fortgang der Zwingli-Ausgabe." ZWA, 11, 1, 1959, 61-63.

984. _____. "Das Gespräch mit den Wiedertäufern am 22. Januar 1528 zu Bern." ZWA, 5, 9, 1933, 409-413.

985. _____. "Die grosse Zwingli-Ausgabe." ZWA, 9, 3, Stand von Mai 1950, 181-182.

986. _____. "Huldreich Zwinglis Sämtliche Werke. Ein Zwischenbericht." ZWA, 12, 1, 1964, 1-9.

987. _____. "Italienischer Humanismus und Zwinglis Reformation." ZWA, 10, 6, 1956, 398-408.

988. _____. "Die Landeskirche des Kantons Zürich im Wandel der Zeiten." ZWA, 11, 1, 1959, 47-56.

988a. _____. "Das Lutherbild Zwinglis." NZZ, 1933. Nr. 2079.

989. _____. "Die politischen Voraussetzungen der Reformation Zwinglis." NZZ, 1969. Nr. 4.

990. _____. "Probleme der Zwingliforschung." Schweizer Beiträge zur Allgemeinen Geschichte, 4, 1946, 247-267.

#991. _____. "Renaissance und Reformation in der Schweiz." ZWA, 11, 1, 1959, 1-23.

#992.   Muralt, Leonhard von. Stadtgemeinde und
Reformation in der Schweiz. Zurich, 1930.
R: W. Köhler, HZ, 143. 1931.

993.   _____. "Über die protestantische Staats-
anschauung." Schweizerische Rundschau, 1937,
393-404. Also: Der Historiker und die Geschichte.
Zurich, 1960. 11-18.

994.   _____. "Ein unbekannter Brief Glareans an
Zwingli." ZWA, 6, 6, 1936, 336-339.

995.   _____. "Von Zwingli zu Pestalozzi." ZWA, 8,
4, 1945, 177-186; ZWA, 9, 6, 1951, 329-364.
Also: Der Historiker und die Geschichte.
Zurich, 1960. 118-140.

996.   _____. "Zum Problem: Reformation und Täufertum."
ZWA, 6, 2, 1934, 65-85.

#997.   _____. "Zum Problem der Theokratie bei Zwingli."
Discordia Concors, Festgabe Edgar Bonjour.
Basel: Helbing and Lichtenhahn, 1968. 369-370.

998.   _____. "Zürichs Beitrag zur Weltgeschichte im
Zeitalter der Reformation." Zürcher Taschenbuch
auf das Jahr 1945. Zurich, 1944.

999.   _____. "Zwingli." NZZ, 1933. Nr. 2399.

1000.   _____. "Zwingli als Begründer der reformierten
Berner Kirche." Mélanges d'histoire et de
littérature offerts a Mr. Charles Gilliard. Lausanne,
1944. 325-330.

#1001.   _____. "Zwingli als Sozialpolitiker." ZWA,
5, 5/6, 1931, 276-296.

1002.   _____. "Zwingli und die Abtei St. Gallen."
Festgabe Hans von Greyerz. Bern: Herbert
Lang, 1967. 295-317.

1003.   _____. "Zwingli und Pestalozzi als Staats-
denker." Archiv für Kulturgeschichte, 34,
1952, 130-153. See also: ZWA, 9, 329-356.

1004.   _____. "Zwinglis-Forschung und Zwingli-
Verein." Mimeographed manuscript distributed
on the occasion of the 450th anniversary of
the Zurich Reformation. Zurich, 1968.
Reprinted: Festschrift Ernst Staehelin, 1969,
137-147.

1005. Muralt, Leonhard von. "Zwinglis Bedeutung für die Gegenwart." Kirchenblatt für die reformierten Gemeinden des Kantons Appenzell a. Rhein, 1931. Nr. 6.

#1006. _____. "Zwinglis dogmatisches Sondergut." ZWA, 5, 7/8, 1932, 321-339, 353-368. Also: Zurich: Beer, 1932.

1007. _____. "Zwinglis geistesgeschichtliche Stellung." NZZ, 1931. Nr. 2052; N. Winterthurer Tagblatt, 1931. Nr. 256; Landbote, 1931. Nr. 474.
   R: W. Köhler, Theologische Rundschau, N.F. 4, 1932.

1008. _____. "Zwinglis Reformation in der Eidgenossenschaft." ZWA, 13, 1, 1969, 19-33.

1009. _____. "Zwinglis Tod, 11. Okt. 1531." Kirchgemeindeblatt von Neumünster, 1931. Nr. 10; Berner Tagblatt, 1931. Nr. 474.

1010. _____. "Zwinglis Tod und Vermächtnis." NZZ, 1931. Nr. 1918.

1011. _____. "Die Zwingli-Stube in der Schulei." ZWA, 5, 8, 1932, 383.

1012. Myconius, Oswald. "Life of Zwingli." The Latin Works of Huldreich Zwingli. Vol. 1. Edited by Samuel M Jackson. Philadelphia: The Heidelberg Press, 1922.

1013. Nabholz, Hans. "Aus Zürichs Geschichte im 15. Jahrhundert." Zürcher Taschenbuch auf das Jahr 1906. Zurich, 1905.

1014. _____. Die Bauernbewegung in der Ostschweiz 1524-1525. 1898. [Bülach dissertation]

1015. _____. "Das politische Erbe des Reformators Ulrich Zwingli." Der Kleine Bund, 1931. Nr. 41.

1016. _____. "Die soziale Schichtung der Bevölkerung der Stadt Zürich bis zu Reformation." Festgabe Max Huber, Zurich: 1934.

89

89

1017. Nabholz, Hans. "Ulrich Zwingli in dramatischer Beleuchtung." Zürcher Taschenbuch auf das Jahr 1912. Zurich, 1911. 99-126. [*]

1018. _____. "Der Zusammenhang der eidgenössischen Bünde mit der gleichzeitigen deutschen Bündnispolitik." Festschrift Meyer von Knonau. Zurich, 1913.

1019. Näf, R. A. "U. Zwingli, réformateur et patriote." Étrennes chrétiennes. 3e année. Geneva, 1876.

1020. _____. "Zum 400. Jahrestag der Schlacht bei Kappel." Anzeiger a. d. Bezirk Affoltern, 1931. Nr. 116.

1021. Nagel, Ernst. "Die Abhängigkeit der Coverdalebibel von der Zürcherbibel." ZWA, 6, 8, 1937, 437-457.

1022. _____. Huldreich Zwingli, ein kirchliches Spiel. Zum 400jähr. Todestag des Zürcher Reformators. Zurich: In Kommission beim Wanderer-Verlag, 1931. [*]

1023. _____. Ein kleines Zwingli-Spiel. Zurich: Zwingli Verlag, 1942. [*]

1024. Neander, J. A. Vitae quattuor Reformatorum: Luther, a Melanchthone, Melanchthonis a Camerario, Zwinglii a Myconio, Calvini a Theodore Beza Conscriptae. Berlin, 1841.

1025. Németh, Balázs. "Zwingli. Ein Lebensbild." Das Wort, 1971/2, September/October, 1, 7-15.

1026. "Ein neues Rütlilied und Zwinglis Ruf nach Zürich." Zurich, 1946. [*]

1027. Neuser, Wilhelm H. "Ein Zwingli-Autograph aus dem Jahre 1526." ZWA, 12, 7, 1967, 533-534.

1028. Newman, Louis I. Jewish Influence on Christian Reform Movements. New York, 1925. 454-510.

1029. Nicolas, Michel. "Zwingli." Nouvelle
Biographie, 45, 1866, pp. 1036 ff.

1030. Niebergall, Alfred. "Über Zwingli als Prediger."
Die Geschichte der christlichen Predigt: III
Leiturgia, Handbuch des evangelischen Gottes-
dienstes, II. Kassel, 1955. 279-282.

1031. Niesel, Wilhelm. "Zwinglis spätere Sakraments-
anschauung." Theologische Blätter, 11, 1932,
Nr. 1.
    R: Fritz Blanke, Theologische Blätter, 11,
    1932; W. Köhler, Theologische Rundschau, N.F.
    4, 1932.

1032. Nolte, Ernst. "Zwinglis Entwicklung zum
Reformator." Lüneburger Gemeindeblatt,
1931. Nr. 20.

1033. _____. "Zwinglis Wirken und Tod als Reformator."
Lüneburger Gemeindeblatt, 1931. Nr. 21.

1034. Nuesch, Alexandes. "Zwinglifeier 1919."Zurich,
1919.

1035. Ochninger, Friedr. "Ulrich Zwingli." Geschichte
des Christentums. New York, 1897. pp. 309 ff.

1036. Odermatt, Arnold. "Eine Ergänzung und zwei
Berichtigungen zu Huldreich Zwinglis Sämtlichen
Werken I." ZWA, 12, 7, 1967, 535-539.

1037. _____. "Weitere Anmerkungen und Berichtigungen
zu Zwinglis Sämtlichen Werken I." ZWA, 12,
10, 1968, 712-715.

1038. _____. "Weitere Erläuterungen zum Text von
Huldrich Zwinglis Sämtlichen Werken I."
ZWA, 13, 4, 1970, 245-254.

1039. Odložilík, O. "Der Widerhall der Lehre Zwinglis
in Mähren." ZWA, 4, 9, 1925, 257-276.

#1040. Oechsli, Wilhelm. "Zwingli als Staatsmann."
Ulrich Zwingli: Zum Gedächtnis der Zürcher
Reformation 1519-1919. Zurich: Berichthaus,
1919.
    R: W. Köhler, Theologische Rundschau, N.F. 4,
    1932.

1041. Oechsli, Wilhelm. "Zwingli als Stifter
      unserer Hochschule." Schweiz. Pädagog.
      Zeitschrift, 1919. Nr. 1.

1042. Oehler, Gustav. "Huldreich Zwingli,
      gest. 11. Okt. 1531, zu s. 400. Todestag
      am 11. Okt. 1931." Evang. Gemeindeblatt, Ulm,
      1931. Nr. 10A.

#1043. Oorthuys, Gerardus. De Anthropologie van
       Zwingli. Leiden: E. J. Brill, 1905.
       R: ZWA, 2, 3, 1906, 94; W. Köhler, ThL,
       32, 1907, 14.

1044. _____. Kruispunten op ten Weg der Kerk:
      Zwingli, De Lavadie, Kohlbrugge. Wageningen:
      H. Veenmanzonen, 1935.

#1045. _____. "Uitleggen en gronden der stellingen."
       Troffel en Zwaard, 1, 1909-1911.

1046. Orelli, Caspar von. "Züge aus der Lebensgeschichte
      Ulrich Zwinglis." Neujahrsblatt der Gesell-
      schaft der Herren Gelehrten auf der Chorherren,
      13, 1791.

1047. Otte, Fr. "Der Zwinglibaum." Die Schweizerische
      Land, Volk und Geschichte in ausgewählten
      Dichtungen. Bern, 1859. 16-17. [*]

1048. Papillon-Rothen, Micheline. Étude comparative
      de la sainte cène chez Luther et Zwingli.
      Geneva, 1953. [Geneva Bachelor's thesis]

1049. Pauck, Wilhelm. "Zwingli, Ulrich." The
      Encyclopedia Americana. Vol. 29. New York:
      Americana Corporation, 1968. 826-827.

1050. Paulus, Nikolaus. "Hexenjage bei den Zwinglianern."
      Historisch-politischen Blättern, 144.

1051. _____. "Die Sittenstrenge der echten Zwinglianer."
      Wissenschaftliche Beilage zur "Germania," 1909.
      Nr. 17.
      R: W. Köhler, ZWA, 2, 12, 1910, 385-386.

1052. _____. "Über Zwinglis Lebenswandel." Der
      Katholik, 1895, p. 175 ff.

92

1053. Paulus, Nikolaus. "Zwingli und die Glaubensfrei-
heit." historisch-politische Blätter 144,
1909.

1054. _____. "Zwingli und die Toleranz." Wissen-
schaftliche Beilage zur "Germania", 1909.
Nr. 17.

1055. Persius, Konrad. Huldreich Zwingli. Barmen:
Hugo Klain, n.d.

#1056. Pestalozzi, Theodor. Die Gegner Zwinglis am
Grossmünsterstift in Zürich. Schweizer
Studien zur Geschichtswissenschaft, II.
Zurich: Gebr. Leemann & Co., 1918.
R: W. Köhler, NZZ, 1918. Nr. 1055;
W. Köhler, ThL, 44, 1919, 248.

1057. Peyer, H. C. "Staat und Kirche in Zürich von
der Reformation bis in die Gegenwart."
Mimeographed manuscript distributed during the
celebration of the 450th anniversary of the
Zürich Reformation. Zürich, 1968.

1058. Die Pfarrbücher der Stadt Zürich 1525-1875 in
Stadtarchiv Zürich. Zürich, 1916.
R: Gerold Meyer von Knonau, ZWA, 3, 9,
1917, 287.

1059. Pfender, Ch. "Zwingli: (Ulrich ou Huldreich)."
La Grande Encyclopédie. Vol 31. Paris:
Librairie Larousse, n.d. 4342-4343.

1060. Pffenninger, Arthur. "Der letzte Tag; ein
Gedenkspiel zum 11. Okt. 1931." Zurich:
Wanderer-Verlag, 1931. [*]

1061. Pfenninger, Heinrich. "Kriegstechnisches
zur Schlacht bei Kappel; von einem Büchsen-
schmied." Zürichsee-Zeitung, 1931. Nr.
247.

1062. Pfenninger-Stadler, Verena. "Gedanken zur
400jähr. Wiederkehr von Ulrich Zwinglis
Todestag am 11. Okt. 1931." Schweizer
Frauenblatt, 1931. Nrs. 41, 42.

1063. Pfister, Jakob. "Zwingli und der Bauernstand."
      Feierabend, 1919. Nr. 2. Supplement to the
      Allgemeinen Anzeiger vom Zürichsee.

1064. Pfister, Rudolf. "Die Freundschaft zwischen
      Guillaume Farel und Huldrych Zwingli." ZWA,
      8, 7, 1947, 372-389.

1065. _____. "Neue Beiträge zur Zwingli-Forschung."
      ZWA, 9, 8, 1952, pp. 445-452.

#1066. _____. Das Problem der Erbsünde bei Zwingli.
      Quellen und Abhandlungen zur schweizerische
      Reformationsgeschichte, IX. Leipzig:
      M. Heinsius Nachfolger, 1939. [Zurich
      dissertation]
         R: W. Köhler, NZZ, 1939. Nrs. 585, 598;
      W. Bremi, ZWA, 7, 1, 1939, 59-61; Kurt
      Guggisberg, ZKG, 59, 1, 1940, 228.

1067. _____. "Quellen zum zürcherischen Täufertum."
      ZWA, 9, 1953, 525-530.

1068. _____. "Die Reformation Huldrych Zwinglis, 450
      Jahre Reformation im Zürich." Limmattaler
      Tagblatt, 1969. Nr. 12.

#1069. _____. Die Seligkeit erwählter Heiden bei
      Zwingli: Eine Untersuchung zu seiner
      Theologie. Zollikon-Zurich: Ewangel. Verlag.
      1952.
         R: L. von Muralt, ZWA, 10, 6, 1956, 404-408;
      F. Blanke, Kirchenblatt für die reformierte
      Schweiz, 1952, 236-237.

1070. _____. "Von Zwinglis Ideen, die heute noch
      leben." Kirchenbote für die evangelisch-
      reformierten Kirchen Basel-Stadt, Glarus,
      Schaffhausen und der Diaspora der Zentral-
      schweiz und im Kanton Solothurn, January 1969,
      1, 1-2.

1071. _____. "Zur Begründung der Seligkeit von
      Heiden bei Zwingli." Evang. Missionsmagazin,
      95, 1951, 70-80.

1072. _____. "Zürich und das anglikanische Staats-
      kirchentum." ZWA, 10, 4, 1955, 249-256.

1073. _____. "Zwingli als Liturg." Der Grundriss,
      5, 1943, 322-329.

1074. Pfister, Rudolf. "Zwingli der Staatsmann."
Zurich, Zwingli-Verlag, 1942.

1074a. _____. "Zwingli, Huldrych (Ulrich)." Evangelisches
Kirchenlexicon. Vol. III. Tübingen, 1960. Cols.
1952-1960.

#1075. _____. "Die Zwingli-Forschung seit 1945.
Forschungsbericht." Archiv, 1957, 2,
230-246.

1076. _____. "Zwingli-Stätten in Zürich." Mimeographed
manuscript distributed on the occasion of the
450th anniversary of the Zurich Reformation.
Zurich, 1968.

1077. Philipp, Eduard. "Huldreich Zwingli; der
reform. Jugend dargeboten." Leipzig, 1931.

1078. _____. "Zwingli und seine Stellung zur Kirchen-
musik." Deutscher Organisten-Kalender, 6,
1931.

1079. _____. "Zwingli; ein Volks- und Gemeindeabend."
Herford and Leipzig, 1931.

1080. Pinson, William, Jr. "Huldrych Zwingli."
20 Centuries of Great Preaching. Vol. II:
Luther to Massillon 1483-1742. Edited by
Clyde E. Fant, Jr. and William M. Pinson,
Jr. Waco, Texas: Word Books, 1971. 77-85.

1081. Pipkin. H. Wayne. The Nature and Development
of the Zwinglian Reformation to August, 1524.
Hartford, 1968. [Hartford dissertation]

1082. _____. "The Preaching and Sermons of Huldrych
Zwingli." 20 Centuries of Great Preaching.
Vol. II: Luther to Massillon 1483-1742.
Edited by Clyde E. Fant, Jr. and William M.
Pinson, Jr. Waco, Texas: Word Books, 1971.
85-91.

1083. _____. "A Synopsis of the Thought of Huldreich
Zwingli as Found in the Three Royal Treatises."
An Analysis of the Institutes of the Christian
Religion. By Ford Lewis Battles. Hartford,
1966. 2nd ed.: Pittsburgh, 1970.

1084. Pipkin, H. Wayne. "Zwingli the Educator."
A History of Religious Educators. Edited
by Elmer Towns. Grand Rapids, Mich.:
Baker Book House.

1085. _____. "Zwingli, the laity and the orders;
from the cloister into the world." Hartford
Quarterly, 8, Winter 1968, 32-41.

1086. Planta, Gaudenz von. "Ulrich Zwingli." Der
erste Flug, Gedichte. Zurich, 1909. 43.
See also: Gedichte. Horgen, 1927, 37. [*]

1087. Poll, G. J. van der. "De Pronaeus in verband
met Zwingli's liturgie." Kerk en Eredienst,
10, 1955, 88-92.

1088. Pollet, Jacques V. Huldrych Zwingli et la
Réforme en Suisse d'après les recherches récentes.
Paris: Presses Universitaires de France,
1963.
    R: R. Stupperich, Archiv, 56, 2, 1965,
    269-270; J. Rogge, ThL, 91, January 1966,
    56-58; J. Staedtke, ThZ, 21, Sept./Oct.
    1965, 457-458; F. Wendel, RHPR, 43, 4,
    1963, 398; O. Vasella, ZSKG, 58, 1964,
    147-148; F. Blanke, NZZ, 1964. Nr. 2352.

1089. _____. "Recherches sur Zwingli A propos
d'ouvrages recents." Revue des sciences
religieuses, 1954, 155-174.

1090. _____. "Zwingli, Huldrych." Lexicon für
Theologie und Kirche. Freiburg: Herder, 1965.

#1091. _____. "Zwinglianisme." Dictionnaire de
théologie catholique. Vol. 15. Paris:
Letouzey et Ané, 1950. 3925-3928.
    R: W. Joest,ZKG, 63, 2, 1950/51, 219-221.

1092. Pongracz, Jozsef. "Zwingli az ember." Dunantuli
protestans lap, 43. Nr. 1-3.

1093. Potter, G. R. "Zwingli and Calvin." The
Reformation Crisis. Edited by Joel Hurstfield.
New York: Harper & Row, 1966. 32-43.

96

1094.   Potter, G. R.   "Zurich and the Reformation in
        Switzerland." History Today, 15, January
        1965, 12-19.

1094a. Powys, Llewelyn, "Zwingli," Swiss Essays. London:
        John Lane, 1947. 131-137

1095.   Pratt, Melvyn Eugene. Zwinglianism in England
        During the Reign of Elizabeth. Stanford,
        1954. [Stanford dissertation]

1096.   Probst, Jacob. "Zum Zwingli-Denkmal, 25.
        Aug. 1885." Aus dem Wanderbüchlein eines
        alten Burschen. Basel: 1912. 162-165. [*]

1097.   Ragaz, Rageth. "Zwingli und wir." Bündner
        Kirchenbote, 1919. Nr. 2.

1098.   Ragaz, Leonhard, "Zwinglis Tod." Neue Weg, 25.
        Nr. 10.

1099.   Rahn, Rudolf. "Ulrich Zwingli an Gerold Meyer
        von Knonau." Neujahrsblatt der Gesellschaft
        der Herren Gelehrten auf der Chorherren, 6,
        1784.

#1100. Ramp, Ernst. Die Stellung von Luther, Zwingli
        und Calvin zur Zinsfrage. Zurich: Zwingli
        Verlag, 1949. [Zurich dissertation]

1101.   _____. Das Zinsproblem. Eine historische
        Untersuchung. Quellen und Abhandlungen zur
        Geschichte des schweizerischen Protestantismus,
        IV. Zurich, 1949.

1102.   Ranck, Henry H. "Zwingli, Reformer and Modern."
        Reformed Church Review, 21, 1917, 25-41.

1103.   Rapp, Eugen Ludwig. Luther, Zwingli, Calvin.
        Kaiserslautern: Evangelische Buchhandlung,
        1953.

1104.   Das reformierte Zürich. Edited by the Kirchenrat
        des Kantons Zürich on the occasion of the 450th
        anniversary of the Zurich Reformation.
        Zurich, 1969.

1105.   Reimann, Hannes. "Huldrych Zwingli der Musiker."
        Archiv für Musikwissenschaft, 17, 1960,
        126-141.

#1106.   Reimann, Hannes. Huldrych Zwingli, der Musiker.
         Allgemeine Musikgesellschaft in Zürich-
         Neujahrsblatt, CXLIV. Zurich: Kommissions-
         verlag, 1960

1107.   Reinhard, E. "Zwingli als Reformator und
         Persönlichkeit." Bund, 1931. Nr. 521.

1108.   Remley, F. A. The Relation of State and Church
         in Zürich 1519 to the first disputation.
         Leipzig, 1895.

1109.   Révész, Imre. "Zwingli." Debreceni Protestans
         Lap. October 22, 1931.

1110.   _____. "Zwingli Ulrik élete, tanitásai,
         jelontösége." Jahrbuch für innere Mission
         der ungar. ev. Kirche Augsb. Konfession,
         1931/32.

1111.   Rhiner, H. "Zwingli und die heilige Johanna."
         Der Kristall, 1931. Nr. 9. Supplement to the
         N. Bündner Zeitung.

1112.   Ribi, Adolf. "Ulrich Zwingli, Staatsmann und
         Prophet." NZZ, 1937. Nr. 2363.

#1113.   Rich, Arthur. Die Anfänge der Theologie
         Huldrych Zwinglis. Quellen und Abhandlungen
         zur Geschichte des schweizerischen Protestantis-
         mus, VI. Zurich: Zwingli-Verlag, 1949.
            R: F. Wendel, Revue d'histoire et de philo-
                sophie religieuses, 30, 1950, p. 354 f.;
                G. W. Richards, TT, 7, January 1951,
                544-54; J. W. Leitch, SJT, 6, December
                1953, 443-445.

#1114.   _____. "Zwingli als sozialpolitischer
         Denker." ZWA, 13, 1, 1969, 67-89. See also:
         Reformatio, 18, January 1969, 9-13; Zeitschrift
         für evangelische Ethik, 13, September 1969,
         257-273; Zeitschrift für öffentliche Fürsorge
         1969, 3, 33-36.

#1115.   _____. "Zwinglis Weg zur
         Reformation." ZWA, 8, 9, 1948, 511-535.

1116. Richards, George W. "Zwingli and the Reformed Tradition." Protestantism. By William K. Anderson. Nashville, 1944.

1117. _____. "Zwingli, Huldreich." Collier's Encyclopedia. Vol. 23. New York: Crowell-Collier Educational Corporation, 1968. 784-785.

1118. Richardson, Cyril Charles. Zwingli and Cranmer on the Eucharist. M. Dwight Johnson Memorial Lectureship in Church History. Evanston, Ill.: Seabury Western Theological Seminary, 1949.
      R: R. H. Nichols, Union Seminary Quarterly Review, 5, May 1950, 47-48.

1119. Rieber, Stadtpfarrer. "Zwei Autographen Zwinglis in der ev. Kirchenbibliothek in Isny." ZWA, 1, 11, 1902, 261-263.

1120. Rieker, K. Grundsätze reformierter Kirchenverfassung. Leipzig: Hirschfeld, 1883.

#1121. Rilliet, Jean. Zwingli le troisième homme de la réforme; les temps et les destins. Paris: Fayard, 1959. See also: Zwingli: Third Man of the Reformation. Translated by Harold Knight. Philadelphia: Westminster Press, 1964.
      R: G. Besse, Revue de Théologie et de Philosophie, 11, 1961, 373-374; L. von Muralt, ZWA, 11, 4, 1960, 272-279; G. Fackre, Christian Century, 82, 1965, 1236-1238; Time, 84, July 17, 1964, 56-57; H. C. Porter, Theology, 68, 1965, 256-257; R. Stafford, Hartford Quarterly, 5, Winter 1965, 89; Bard Thompson, JCH, 34, 4, 1965, 463; A.D.L. Reformed and Presbyterian World, 28, 5, 1965, 239-240; M. E. Osterhaven, The Reformed Review, 18, 4, 1965, 52-53.

1122. Rippmann, E. "Unser Zwinglibild." Evang. Gemeindeblatt für Schweizer Diasporagemeinden, 1918/19. Nr. 9.

1123. Ritter, G. "Huldreich Zwingli 1484 bis 1531." Die grossen Deutschen: Neue deutsche Biographie. Vol. 5. Berlin, 1937. 81-90.

99

1124. Rogge, Joachim. "Die Initia Zwinglis und
       Luthers. Eine Einführung in die Probleme."
       Luther Jahrbuch 1963. Hamburg: Friedrich
       Witte Verlag, 1963. 107-133.

#1125. _____. Zwingli und Erasmus. Die Friedens-
       gedanken des jungen Zwingli. Arbeiten
       zur Theologie, XI. Stuttgart: Calwer Verlag,
       1962.

1126. Rollett, Hermann. "Huldreich Zwingli."
       Heldenbilder und Sagen. St. Gallen, 1854.
       p. 137 f.

1127. Rordorf-Gwalter, Sal. "Die Geschwister Rosilla
       und Rudolf Rordorf und ihre Beziehungen zu
       Zürcher Reformatoren." ZWA, 3, 6, 1915,
       180-193.

1128. Rossel, Maurice. "Ulrich Zwingli, 1 janvier
       1484 au 11 oct. 1531, réformateur de Zurich
       et de la Suisse allemande." Bulletin pédagogique
       de la Soc. des instituteurs bernois, 1931.
       28-31.

1129. Rothenberger, A. "Den Manen Ulrich Zwinglis."
       Relig. Volksblatt, 1919. Nr. 1.

#1130. Rother, Siegfried. Die religiösen und geistigen
       Grundlagen der Politik Huldrych Zwinglis; ein
       Beitrag zum Problem des christlichen Staates.
       Erlanger Abhandlungen z. mittleren und neueren
       Geschichte, N.F. VII. Erlangen: Palm &
       Enke, 1956.
           R: H. Gutzwiller, ZSKG, 51, 1957, 244-246.

1131. Rotscheidt, W. "Zwingli-ABC." Reformierte
       Kirchenzeitung, 1933, 407.

1132. Royer, Paul S. "Was hat uns die Zürcher Gedenk-
       feier des 400. Todestages des Reformators
       Huldrych Zwingli am 10. u. 11. Okt. 1931 zu
       sagen?" Evang. Gemeindeblatt, 1931. Nr. 11.

#1133. Rückert, Oskar Ernst. Ulrich Zwinglis Ideen
       zur Erziehung und Bildung in Zusammenhang mit
       seinem reformatorischen Tendenzen dargestellt.
       Gotha: E. F. Thienemann, 1900.

1134. Rudolf, Friedrich. "Die Erstausgaben von Zwinglis Werken 1545." NZZ, 1945. Nrs. 941, 946.

1135. Rüegg, A. "Huldreich Zwingli." Der Kirchenfreund, 1919. Nr. 1.

1136. Rüegg, Ferdinand. "Zwingli in Wien." ZSKG, 2, 1908, 214-219.

1137. _____. "Zwinglis Ausschluss von der Wiener Universität." ZSKG, 5, 1911, 241-260.

1138. Rüegg, Heinrich. "Huldreich Zwingli." Landbote und Tagblatt der Stadt Winterthur, 1918.

1139. Rüegg, Walter. "Zwinglis Stellung zur Kunst." Reformatio, 6, 1957, 271-282.

1140. Ruoff, W. "The descendants of Ulrich Zwingli, the Reformer." The Utah genealogical and historical magazine, 28, 1937, 1, 19-24; 2, 69-74; 3.

1141. _____. "Ein Fall von Nachrichtendienst im Zweiten Kappelerkrieg." ZWA, 11, 1960, 217-218.

1142. _____. Nachfahren Ulrich Zwinglis mit einer vorläufigen Nachfahrenliste. Schweizerische Gesellschaft für Familienforschung.Veröffentlichungen, V. Bern, Weihnachten, 1937.

#1143. Rupp, E. G. "The Reformation in Zurich, Strassburg and Geneva." The New Cambridge Modern History. Vol. II: The Reformation 1520-59. Edited by G. R. Elton. Cambridge: Cambridge University Press, 1968, 96-119.

1143a. Rüsch, E. G. "Die Erziehungsgrundsätze Huldreich Zwinglis." Von Heiligen in der Welt. Zollikon, 1959, 72-98.

1144. _____. "Gelöstes Rätsel um einen Zwingli-Brief." ZWA, 12, 9, 1968, 665-667.

#1145. _____. "Die humanistischen Vorbilder der Erziehungsschrift Zwinglis." ThZ, 22, 1966, 126-147. R: B. Moeller, HZ, 205, August 1907, 213.

1146. _____. "Zwingli und Luther." Reformiertes Kirchenblatt, 46, March 1969, 2-3, 9.

1147. Rüsch, E. G. "Zwinglis Verhältnis zu Luther."
      Landbote, 1969. Nr. 4.

1148. Rüsch, T. "Aus dem Leben von Theologie und
      Kirche." Reformatio, 18, February 1969,
      124-129.

1149. Rütlinger, Johann Jakob. "Auf Zwinglis
      Reformationsfeyer den 3 January 1819."
      Ländliche Gedichte. Vol. II.Ebnat, 1824.
      62-65. [*]

1150. _____. "Nachruf auf Zwingli, auf seinem
      Sterbefeld bei Kappel." Ländliche Gedichte.
      Vol. I. Ebnat, 1823. 25-28. [*]

1151. _____. "Zwingli Hüsli 1816." Ländliche
      Gedichte. Vol. III. Ebnat, 1826. 82-85. [*]

1152. Sax, Karl. "Zwingli." Wissen und Leben, 11, 1917
      129. See also: Religiöses Volksblatt, 1919,
      2, 12. Karl, Sax, Dichtung. Zurich, 1928. 50.[*]

1153. Sch. P. "Neujahr 1519." NZZ, 1919. 1.

1154. Schaarschmidt, F. "Die Persönlichkeit des
      früher sog. Zwingli in den Uffizien."
      Repertorium für Kunstwissenschaft, 23,
      1900, 3, pp. 222 ff.

1155. Schädelin, Albert. "Zwingli." Bern: A
      Francke, 1919.

1156. Schäfer, Wilhelm. Huldreich Zwingli. Ein
      deutsches Volksbuch. Stuttgart: Verl.
      Deutsche Volksbücher, 1952.

1157. _____. Huldreich Zwingli. Ein epischer Versuch.
      Weimar: Gesellschaft der Bibliophilen, 1927.[*]

1158. _____. "Huldreich Zwingli; zum 400. Tag
      seines Todes: 11. Okt." Frankfurter Zeitung,
      October 11, 1931.

#1159. Schaff, Philip. "The Theology of Zwingli."
      Reformed Quarterly Review, 36, 1889, 423-431.

1160. Schaufelberger, Walter. "Kappel
       Die Hintergründe einer militärischen Katastrophe."
       Schweizerisches. Archiv für Volkskunde, 51, 1/2,
       1955, 34-61.

1161. Schedler, R. "Ulrich Zwinglis Werdegang."
       Schweiz. Reformblätter, 1919. Nr. 1.

1162. Scheler, Siegmund. "An Zwinglis Hütte zu
       Wildenhaus im Toggenburg." Herzensergüsse.
       Erlangen, 1819. 138. [*]

1163. Scherrer, Gustav. Getreu bis in den Tod;
       historisches Drama aus der Zürcher Reformations-
       geschichte, 1522-1527. Zurich: G. Scherrer,
       1953. [*]

1164. Schiess, T. "Jakob Salzmann, ein Freund
       Zwinglis aus älterer Zeit." ZWA, 1, 8,
       1900, 167-174.

1165. Schinz, Johann Heinrich. "Ulrich Zwingli und
       die Verbreitung der Bibel." Neujahrsblatt der
       Gesellschaft auf den Chorrherren, 38, 1816.

1166. Schlaginhaufen, Otto. "Anthropologische
       Bemerkungen zu Dürers 'Zwingli'Bildnis'."
       NZZ, 1948. Nr. 2724.

1167. Schlatter, Theodor. "Zwingli's Theocracy. Robert
       C. Walton, University of Toronto Press, 1967.
       Replik zur Besprechung von Martin Haas.
       (Zwingliana 1970 nr. 1 s. 214 f.)"
       Mimeographed manuscript in folder Da2140.35,
       Staatsarchiv, Zurich.

1168. Schmid, Alfred. "Kein zyt ist geschickter guots
       ze tuon, dann die Jugend." Schaffhauser
       Intelligenzblatt, 1931. Nr. 238.

1169. _____. "Zwingli und unsere Kirche." Schaffhauser
       Intelligenzblatt, 1931. Nr. 238.

1170. Schmid, Ernst. "Het man ihm do gvolgt, wer
       unss vor vil Schaden gsin. [Huldrych Zwingli
       und die Schlacht von Marignano]" Sonntagsblatt
       d. Basler Nachrichten, 1944. Nr. 36.

1171. Schmid, Ernst. "Zwingli und Glarus." NZZ, 1944. Nrs. 1389,1394.

1172. Schmid, Ferdinand. Die Vermittlungsbemühungen des In- und Auslandes während der beiden Kappelerkriege. Basel, 1946. [Zurich dissertation]

1173. Schmid, Hans Rudolf. "Den Zwingli lass ich nicht im Stich." Limmataler Tagblatt, 1931. Nr. 227.

#1174. Schmid, Heinrich. Zwinglis Lehre von der göttlichen und menschlichen Gerechtigkeit. Studien z. Dogmengeschichte und systematischen Theologie, XII. Zurich: Zwingli Verlag, 1959. [Zurich dissertation]
    R: P. Scherding, RHPR, 43, 1963, 2, 204-205; Paul Jacobs, ThL, 85, 1960, 290-292; H. Sasse, Reformed Theological Review, 19, 3, 1960, 87-88.

1175. Schmid, Martin. "Ulrich Zwingli; zu s. 400. Todestag." Der Kristall, 1931. Nr. 10. Supplement to the N. Bündner Zeitung.

1176. Schmid, Walter. "Johannes Stumpfs Schweizer- und Reformationschronik." ZWA, 10, 8, 1957, 502-506.

1177. Schmidt, "Zwingli und das Wort Gottes." Der Geisteskampf der Gegenwart, 1931. Nr. 11.

#1178. Schmidt-Clausing, Fritz. "Das Corpus Juris Canonici als reformatorisches Mittel Zwinglis." ZKG, 80, 1, 1969, 14-21.

1179. _____. "Die Entdeckung des echten Zwingli." ThL, 93, March 1968, 169-172.

1180. _____. "Huldrych Zwingli; zum 480. Geburtstag, 1. Jan 1964." Gemeindeblatt der Heilsbronnen, Berlin, January 1, 1964, 1-3.

1181. _____. "Johann Ulrich Surgant, ein Wegweiser des jungen Zwingli." ZWA, 11, 5, 1961, 287-320.

1182. Schmidt-Clausing, Fritz. "Die Neudatierung der Liturgischen Schriften Zwinglis." ThZ, 25, July/August 1969, 252-265.

#1183. _____. "Das Prophezeigebet. Ein Blick in Zwinglis Liturgische Werkstatt. Aus den Vorarbeiten zu den 'Theologischen Grundlagen der Zwinglischen Liturgie'." ZWA, 12, 1964, 10-34.

1184. _____. "Die unterschiedliche Stellung Luthers und Zwinglis zum Jakobusbrief." Reformatio, 18, October 1969, 658-585.

#1185. _____. Zwingli. Berlin: Walter de Gruyter, 1965.
R: R. Stupperich, Archiv, 58, 2, 1967, 263-264; Ernst Rusch, ZWA, 12, 5, 1966, 371-372; R. Pfister ThL, 92, March 1967, 207-208; Max Schoch, NZZ, 1965. Nr. 1714; Oskar Vasella, ZSKG, 59, 1965, 250-252.

#1186. _____. Zwingli als Liturgiker. Eine liturgiegeschichtliche Untersuchung. Veröffentlichungen d. evangel. Geschichte für Liturgieforschung, VII. Göttingen: Evangelischen Gesellschaft, 1952.
R: Rudolf Pfister, ZWA, 9, 9, 1953, pp. 558 ff.; M. Jenny, ThZ, 11, November/December, 1965, 468-472; Leonhard Fendt, ThL, 78, 1953, 293-295. G. W. Locher, Musik und Gottesdienst, 9, 1955.

1187. _____. "Zwingli und die Kindertaufe." Berliner Kirchen-Briefe, 1962, 6, 4-8.

#1188. _____. Zwinglis Humor. Frankfurt: Otto Lembeck, 1968.
R: M. Jenny, Reformatio, 8, April 1969, 263-264; Kirchenbote für die evangelisch-reformierten Kirchen Basel-Stadt, Glarus, Schaffhausen und der Diaspora der Zentralschweiz und im Kanton Solothurn, January 1969. Nr. 1. M. Haas, ZWA, 13, 7, 1972, 488-489.

#1189. _____. Zwinglis Kanonversuch. Frankfurt: Otto Lembeck, 1969. M. Haas, ZWA, 13, 7, 1972, 489.

#1190. _____. Zwinglis liturgische Formuläre. Frankfurt: Otto Lembeck, 1970.
R. M. Haas, ZWA, 13, 7, 1972, 489-490.

#1191. Schmidt-Clausing, Fritz. "Zwinglis Stellung zum Konzil." ZWA, 11, 8, 1962, 479-498.

1192. Schneider, Arthur. "Zwinglis Frau; Erinnerungs- blatt z. 400. Wiederkehr des Todestages des Reformators, 11. Okt. 1531." Reformierte Kirchenzeitung, Wupperthal, 1931. Nr. 39.

1193. Schneider, Hugo. "Die Zwingli-Waffen." NZZ, 1948. Nrs. 115, 117.

1195. Schnyder, Werner. "Auf den Spuren von Ulrich Zwinglis Grossvater." ZWA, 7, 1939, 57-59.

1196. Schnyder, Wilhelm. "Ulrich Zwingli; z. 400. Jahrestage s. Todes." Vaterland, 1931. Nr. 239. Also: Acht Studien z. Christl. Altertwissen. u. z. Kirchengeschichte, 1937, 79-89.

1197. Schoch, Max. "Die Einheit von Kirche und Staat bei Zwingli." NZZ, 1969. Nr. 4.

1198. Schönholzer, Gottfried. "Zum 11. Oktober." Der Protestant, 21, 1918, 21, 83.

1199. _____. "Zwingli als Prediger und Seelsorger." Der Protestant, 1918. Nr. 26.

#1200. Schrenk, D. G. "Zwinglis Hauptmotiv in der Abendmahlslehre und das Neue Testament." ZWA, 5, 4, 1930, 176-185.

1201. Schubert, H. von. "Die Vorgeschichte des Marburger Gesprächs." ZKG, 29, 1908, 323-342.

1202. _____. "Das Marburger Gespräch als Anfang der Abendmahlskonkordie." ZKG, 30, 1909, 60-78.

1203. Schuli, M. "Zwinglis besondere Grösse als Reformator." Der Protestant, 1918. Nr. 26. See also: Evang. Kirchenbote für den Kanton Thurgau, 1919. Nr. 2.

1204. Schulthess, J. Georg. "Zwinglis Hütte." Helvetischer Kalender für das Jahr 1797. Zurich, 1797. 43. See also: J. M. Schuler, Huldreich Zwingli. Zurich, 1818. 126.

#1205. Schulthess-Rechberg, Gustav von. Luther, Zwingli
        und Calvin in ihren Ansichten über das
        Verhältnis von Staat und Kirche. Zürcher Beiträge
        zur Rechtwissenschaft, XXIV. Zurich: Leeman &
        Cie, 1909.
            R: ZWA, 2, 11, 1910, 349-350.

1206.   _____. "Die Schlacht von Kappel im Kardinals-
        kollegium." ZWA, 2, 1911, 434-439.

1207.   Schulz, Friedrich. Zwinglis Abschied, 10
        Oktober 1531. St. Gallen, 1916. [*]

1208.   Schwalb, Maurice. Étude comparative des doctrines
        de Melanchthon, Zwingle et Calvin. Paris &
        Strassbourg, 1859.

1209.   Schwarz, D. "Hat Dürer Zwingli gemalt?"
        NZZ, 1948. Nr. 1676.

1210.   Schwarz, D. W. H. Die Statutenbücher der Propstei
        St. Felix und Regula (Grossmünster) zu Zürich.
        Zurich: Schulthess & Co., 1952.
            R: Theodor Mayer, HZ, 177, February 1954, 189.

1211.   Schwarz, Rudolf. "Huldrych Zwingli." Baselbieter
        Kirchenbote, 1919. Nr. 1.

1212.   _____. "Das tragische Ende Huldrych Zwinglis."
        Sonntagsbeilage der National-Zeitung, 1931. Nr.
        470.

1213.   Schweizer, Alexander. Zwinglis Bedeutung Neben
        Luther. Zurich: Schulthess, 1884.

#1214. Schweizer, Julius. Reformierte Abendmahlsgestaltung
        in der Schau Zwinglis. Basel: F. Reinhardt,
        1954. See also: Musik und Gottesdienst, 1954,
        4, 161-171.
            R: Hans Reimann, Musik und Gottesdienst,
            1954, 4, 171-174; Karl Fueter, NZZ, 1954.
            Nr. 2753; N. Winterthurer Tagblatt, 1955.
            Nr. 46.

1216. Schweizer, Julius. "Zur Frage der Restauration von Gotteshäusern in zwinglischem Gebiet." ThZ, 12, March/April 1956, 237-252.

1217. _____. Zur Ordnung des Gottesdienstes in den nach Gottes Wort reformierten Gemeinden der deutschsprachigen Schweiz. Kirchliche Zeitfragen, XII. Zurich, 1944.

1218. Schweizer, Paul. "Die Schlacht bei Kappel am 11. Oktober 1531." Jahrbuch für schweizerische Geschichte, 41, 1916, 1-50.
    R: Gerold M. von Knonau, ZWA, 3, 8, 1916, 259-260.

1219. Secretan, Jean. "Ulrich Zwingli; 400e anniversaire." Tribune de Lausanne, October 9, 1931.

1220. Sée, Henri; Rebillon, Armand; Preclin, Edmond. "Luther and Zwingli." Le 16e siècle. Paris, 1942. pp. 147 ff.

1221. Seeberg, Erich. "Der Gegensatz zwischen Zwingli, Schwenckfeld und Luther." Reinhold Seeberg Festschrift. Leipzig, 1929. 43-80.

1222. Seitz, Otto. "Die Stellung des Urbanus Rhegius im Abendmahlsstreit." ZKG, 19, 1898, pp. 293 ff.

1223. _____. Die theologische Entwicklung des Urbanus Rhegius, spez. sein Verhältnis zu Luther und Zwingli in den Jahren 1521-1523. Gotha, 1898. [Halle dissertation]

1224. Sell, Karl. "Zwingli." Aus Religions- und Kirchengeschichte. 7 Vorträge. Darmstadt, 1880. pp. 181 ff.

1225. Senn, Jacques. Chronika des weiland Reiterknechts Ambrosi Schwerter. Vergilbte Blätter aus der Reformationszeit. Bern, 1919.

1226. Sibler, Georg. "Die Folgen des zweiten Kappelerkrieges, Okt.-Nov. 1531." Schweiz. Volksblatt von Bachtel, 1931. Nr. 156. See also: Bülach-Dielsd. Wochenzeitung, 1931. Nr. 81.

1227. Sibler, Georg. "Zwinglis Jugend." Appenzeller
       Zeitung, 1931. Nr. 238.

1228. Sieber, Paul. "Bibliographie zur Zwingli-
       Gedenkfeier des Jahres 1931." ZWA, 5, 8,
       1932, 368-383.

1229. Sieber, Th. "George Staheli und die Reformation
       in Weiningen." ZWA, 3, 9/10, 1917, 277-
       284, 296-305.

1230. Siegfried, André. "Zwingle et le Zwinglianisme."
       Les forces religieuses et la vie politique:
       Le catholicisme et le protestantisme.
       Cahiers de la Fondation nat. des sc. politiques,
       XXIII. Paris: Libr. A. Colin, 1951.

1231. Siegmund-Schultze, Friedrich. "Die evangelischen
       Kirchen der Schweiz." Ekklesia, eine Sammlung
       von Selbstdarstellungen der christlichen
       Kirchen. Vol. III. Gotha, 1935.

1232. Simpson, Samuel. Life of Ulrich Zwingli the
       Swiss Patriot and Reformer. New York:
       Baker & Taylor, 1902.

1233. Smend, Julius, Die evangelischen deutschen
       Messen bis zu Luthers deutscher Messe.
       Göttingen, 1896.

1234. _____. "Eine Wallfahrt nach Wildhaus."
       Die Christliche Welt, 11, 1897, pp. 914 ff.

1235. Soós, Belá von. "Zwingli und Calvin."
       ZWA, 6, 6, 1936, 306-327.

1236. _____. Zwingli és Luther talákorzása Marburgban.
       Debrecen, 1932.

1237. Spach, Ed. "Ulrich Zwingli." Evangelisch-
       protestantischer Kirchenbote für Elsass
       Lothringen, 13, 1884. [*]

#1238. Spillmann, Kurt. "Zwingli und die Zürcher
        Schulverhältnisse." ZWA, 11, 7, 1962,
        427-448.

#1239. Spillmann, Kurt. Zwingli und die zürcherische
        Politik gegenüber der Abtei St. Gallen.
        Mitteilungen zur vaterländischen Geschichte,
        XLIV. St. Gallen, 1965. [Zurich dissertation]
        R: E. G. Rüsch, Archiv, 58, 1, 1967,
        134-135; F. Schmidt-Clausing, ThL, 92,
        January 1967, 51-52; Paul Herzog, ZSKG,
        60, 1966, 317-320; W. Hollenweger, HZ, 205,
        August 1967, 213-214.

#1240. _____. "Zwingli und Zürich nach dem Ersten
        Landfrieden." ZWA, 12, 4, 1965, 254-280; 5,
        1966, 309-329.

#1241. _____. "Zwingli, Zürich und die Abtei St.
        Gallen." Zürcher Taschenbuch auf das Jahr
        1966. Zurich, 1965, 39-61.

1242. _____. "Zwinglis politische Pläne in der
       Ostschweiz." Rorschacher Neujahrsblatt, 52,
       1962, 61-74.

1243. Spinner, Gerhard. "Die Folgen des Kappeler-
       krieges." Lägern-Bote, 1931. Nr. 81. See also:
       Bülach-Dielsdorfer Wochenzeitung, 1931. Nr. 81.

1244. Spinner, Joh. "Wie Zwingli gepredigt hat."
       Gemeindeblatt für die Glieder und Freunde der
       Gemeinde Oberstrass, 1918. Nr. 6.

1245. Spitta, Friedr. "Neue Entdeckungen zum
       Zwingliliede Monatschrift für Gottesdienst
       und kirchl. Kunst, 3, 1898, pp. 22 ff.

1246. _____. "Reformationslied Zwinglis." Monatsschrift
       für Gottesdienst und kirchliche Kunst, 2,
       1897, pp. 196 ff. [*]

1247. Springer, Ludwig. "Huldreich Zwingli, 1.
       Jan. 1484-11. Okt. 1531." Der Türmer,
       October/November 1931.

#1248. Sprüngli, Bernhard. Beschreibung der Kappeler-
        kriege; auf Grund des 1532 verfassten Originals
        erstmals hg. Dr. Leo Weisz. Quellen u.
        Studien z. Gesch. d. helvetischen Kirche, II.
        Zurich: Reform. Bucherstube, 1932. See also:
        Reform. Schweizerzeitung, 1931. Nrs. 39-44.

1249. Staedtke, Joachim. "Das genaue Datum einer
bisher undatierten Schrift Zwinglis." ZWA,
11, 7, 1962, 449-455.

1250. _____. "Eine neue Version des sogenannten
Utinger-Berichtes vom Marburger Religions-
gespräch 1529." ZWA, 10, 4, 1955, 210-
216.

1251. _____. "Voraussetzungen der Schweizer Abendmahlslehre." ThZ, 16, January/February
1960, 19-32.

1252. _____. "Ein wiedergefundenes Original aus
dem Briefwechsel Zwinglis." ZWA, 12, 1,
1964, 78.

1253. Staehelin, Ernst. "Zwei private Publikationen
über die Badener Disputation und ihre
Autoren." ZKG, 37, 1917/18, 378-405.

1254. _____. "Die Zwingliliteratur der Jahre
1913-1920." ZKG, 39, 1922, 166-76.

1255. _____. "Zwinglis Gottesanschauung, Vortrag
an der Christl. Studentenkonferenz in Aarau
1919." NZZ, 1919. Nr. 474.

1256. _____. "Zwinglis Kampf um eine evangel.
Schweiz und sein Tod." Nationalzeitung, October
12, 1931; N. Winterthurer Tagblatt, 1931. Nr. 240.

1257. Staehelin, Rudolf. Der Einfluss Zwinglis auf
Schule und Unterricht. Basel, 1889.

1258. _____. "Huldreich Zwingli." Der Protestantismus
am Ende des 19. Jahrhunderts in Wort und
Bild, 1900, 4, pp. 73 ff.

#1259. _____. Huldreich Zwingli. Sein Leben und
Wirken. 2 vols. Basel: Benno Schwabe Verlag, 1895, 1897,
R: Th. Kolde, ZKG, 17, 1897, 317-318;
Max Staub, NZZ, 1898. Nr. 6.

1260. Staub, W. "Die zwingliausstellung in der
Zentralbibliothek Zürich." Kirchenblatt für
die reformierte Schweiz, 1919. pp. 95 ff.

1261. Staub, W. "Zwinglis Bedeutung für die Gegenwart." Kirchenblatt für die reformierte Schweiz, 1919, pp. 19 ff.

1262. _____. "Zwinglis Pestlied." Kirchliches Gemeindeblatt für Wetzikon und Seegraben, 1918. Nr. 14.

1263. Steck, Rudolf; Tobler, Gustav. Aktensammlung zur Geschichte der Berner Reformation, 1521-1532. Bern: Wyss, 1918-1923.
R: W. Köhler, ThL, 45, 1920, 205;
W. Köhler, NZZ, 1920. Nr. 1534; 1923. Nr. 1085.

1264. Steck, Rudolf. "Luthers Bedeutung für die Schweizerische Reformation." ZWA, 3, 10, 1917, 306-314. See also: Protestantische Monatshefte, 21, 7, 1917, 193-200.

1265. _____. "Ursula Tremp, Zwinglis Base." ZWA, 4, 2, 1921, 46.

1266. _____. "Zwingli und Bern." Schweizerische Theologische Zeitschrift, 1919. pp. 2 ff. See also: Blätter für bernische Geschichte, Kunst und Altertumskunde, 1919, 1/2.

1267. Stelzer, Jakob. "Die Schlacht bei Kappel, 11. Okt. 1531." Zürichsee Zeitung, 1931. Nr. 235.

1268. Stern, Alfred. "'Doctor Jesus' in Zwinglis Briefwechsel." ZWA, 2, 12, 1910, 355-356.

1269. Stickelberger, Emanuel. "Deutschschweizerische Reformatoren." Beth-El, 1932, 11.

1270. _____. "Der Feldprediger." Die verborgene Hand, Schattenrisse zur Geschichte. Stuttgart, 1932. 219-226.

1271. _____. "Die träfe Wahrheit." Gedichte. Zurich, 1929. 48. [*]

1272. _____. Zwingli. Zurich: Grethlein & Co., 1925. [*]
R: Walther Meier, ZWA, 4, 11, 1926, 345-346;
See: Rudolf Schröder, Sonntagsblatt d. Basler Nachrichten, 1954. Nr. 11.

112

1273. Stickelberger, Emanuel. "Zwingli als Feldprediger."
NZZ, 1931. Nr. 1918.

1274. _____. "Zwinglis Kampf um Kirche und Volk."
Der Tag, October 11, 1931.

1275. _____. "Zwinglis Tod auf dem Schlachtfeld
zu Kappel." Schweizerische reformierte
Volksblatt, 1931. Nr. 41.

1276. Stickelberger, Rudolf. "450 Jahre Zürcher
Reformation: Vom Leutpriest zum Reformator."
Woche, 1969. Nr. 3.

1277. Stiller, Otto. Luther und Zwingli. Vergleich
hinsichtlich ihres Entwicklungsganges und
der Art ihres Wirkens. Gotha: Thienemann,
1913.
   R: W. Köhler, Theologische Rundschau, 17,
   1914.

1278. Stober, Adolf. "Zwinglis Denkstein bei Kappel."
Reisebilder aus der Schweiz. Basel, 1850.
91-93. See also: Reformationslieder.
Basel, 1857. 38-40. [*]

1279. _____. "Zwingli am Feste der Engelweihe
zu Einsiedeln." Reformationslieder. Basel,
1857. 33-37. [*]

1280. Stockmeyer, Karl. Bilder aus der Schweizerischen
Reformations-Geschichte zum 400 jährigen
Reformations-Jubiläum 1517. Basel: Frobenius,
1917.
   R: Gerold Meyer von Knonau, ZWA, 3, 9,
   1917, 288.

1281. Stolz, Joh. Jak. "Zwingli als Feldprediger in
Monza 1515." Zurich, 1819.

1282. Straehle, Julius. "Zwingli in der Schlacht bei
Kappel." Schweizer Evangelist, 1931. Nr. 41. [*]

1283. Strasser, Otto Erich. "Zwingli; Säkularerinnerung
an s. Todestag." Berner Tagblatt, November
16, 1931.

1284. Strickler, Gustav. "Die Schlacht bei Kappel
am 11. Okt. 1531." Schweizer Wochenzeitung,
1931. Nr. 38.

1285. Strickler, Gustav. "Zwingli als Staatsmann."
       Der Freisinnige, 1931. Nr. 101.

1286. _____. "Das Zwingli-Denkmal in Zürich."
       NZZ, 1931. Nr. 1496.

1287. Strohl, H. La Pensée de la Réforme. Neuchâtel
       & Paris: Delachaux, 1951.

1288. _____. "La Réforme en Suisse." Revue d'histoire
       et de philosophie religieuses, 23, 1943,
       55-79.

1289. _____. "Zwingle prédicateur." Revue d'histoire
       et de philosophie religieuses, 25, 1945,
       41-51.

1290. Stucki, A. "Anna Reinhard. Die Gattin Zwinglis
       1487-1538." Appenzeller Sonntagsblatt, 1954,
       91-92, 99-100, 107-108, 115-116, 123-124.

1291. Studer, Julius. "Der Schulmeister Johannes
       Buchstab von Winterthur, ein Gegner Zwinglis."
       Schweizerische Theologische Zeitschrift,
       1912, 5.

#1292. Stumpf, Johannes. Chronica vom Leben und Wirken
       des Ulrich Zwingli. Edited by Leo Weisz.
       Quellen und Studien zur Geschichte der helvetischen
       Kirche, I. Zurich: Reformierte Bücherstube,
       1932.
          R: W. Köhler, Theologische Rundschau,
       N.F. 4, 1932; Zeitschrift für die Geschichte
       des Oberrheins, N.F. 46, 1933; Religiöse
       Volksblätter, 63. Nr. 3; Diethelm Fretz,
       ZWA, 5, 10, 1933, 458-459.

#1293. _____. Schweizer- und Reformationschronik. 2 vols.
       Edited by Ernst Gagliardi, Hans Müller and
       Fritz Büsser. Allgemeine Geschichtforschende
       Gesellschaft der Schweizerischen Quellen zur
       Schweizer Geschichte, V, VI. Basel: Birkhauser,
       1953, 1955.
          R: Walther Schmid, ZWA, 10, 8, 1957,
       502-506; O. Vasella, ZSKG, 48, 1954, 210-212;
       O. Vasella, ZSKG, 52, 1958, 261-263; R.
       Pfister, ThL, 82, 1957, 858-859.

1294. Stumpf, "Zwinglis Tod." Volkskalender für
die reformierte Schweiz und ihre Diaspora
1934, 12, 1934.

1295. Stupperich, Robert. "Die Zwingli- und Calvin-
Forschung der letzten zwei Jahrzehnten im
deutschen Sprachgebiet." Archiv für Kulturgeschichte, 42, 1960, 108-126.

1296. Sutter, Will. "Zwingli und unsere Generation.
Eine Panoptikum ohne Kommentar." Kirchenbote
für den Kanton Zürich, 55, 1969, 5.[*]

1297. Sutz, Johannes. "Huldrych Zwingli als Volksmann."
Der Protestant, 1919. pp. 29 ff. See also:
"Die Pestalozzifeier." NZZ, 1919. Nr. 30.

1298. _____. "Zwingli und das Vaterland."
Gemeindeblatt für die Glieder und Freunde
der St. Petersgemeinde, 1918. Nr. 6.

1299. _____. "Zwinglis Tod." Religiöses Volksblatt,
1926, 45, 377.

#1300. Tappolet, Walter. Das Marienlob der Reformatoren:
Martin Luther, Johannes Calvin, Huldrych
Zwingli, Heinrich Bullinger. Tübingen:
Katzmann-Verlag, 1962.

1301. Taylor, Henry Osborn. "Melanchthon and Zwingli."
Thought and Expression in the 16th Century.
Vol. I. New York, 1930. 269-276.

1302. Terray, László. "Kirkkebegrepet hos Zwingli
omkring 1525." Tidsskrift for teologi og
Kirke, 21, 4, 1950, 185-196.

1303. Theiling, Hanns. "Leutpriester Huldrych Zwingli;
z. 400. Todestag des Reformators." Zürcher
Illustrierte, 1931. Nr. 41.

1304. Thomas, Wilhelm. Das Erkenntnisprinzip bei
Zwingli. Leipzig: Hofmann, 1902.
R: W. Köhler, ThL, 28, 1903, 146.

1305. Thommen, Rudolf. "Ein früher Anhänger Zwinglis
in Worms." ZWA, 4, 11, 1926, 342-343.

#1306.   Thompson, Bard. "Ulrich Zwingli." Reformers in
         Profile. Edited by B. A. Gerrish. Philadelphia:
         Fortress Press, 1967. 115-141.

#1307.   _____. "Zwingli Study since 1918." JCH, 19,
         1950, 116-128.

1308.   Thürer, Georg. "Der junge Zwingli in Glarus."
         N. Glarner Zeitung, 1931. Nr. 234.

1309.   _____. Meischter Zwingli. Glarus: Tschudi,
         1943. [*]

1310.   Thürer, Paul. "Die Beziehungen zwischen
         Zwingli und Glarus nach dessen Wegzug aus
         Glarus." Die Reformierte Schweiz, 1952, 10,
         292-294.

1311.   Thürlings, A. Die schweizerischen Tonmeister
         im Zeitalter der Reformation. Bern, 1903.

1312.   Tobler, Rudolf. "Am Neujahrsmorgen 1919 im
         Grossmünster." Kirchenbote für den Kanton
         Zürich, 1919. Nr. 2.

1313.   Tobler, Salomon. "Ulrich Zwingli." Lieder
         des Kampfes. Winterthur, 1848. 131-173.
         See also: Schweizerische Nationalbibliothek.
         Edited by Robert Weber. Vol. IX. Aarau, 1885.
         42-67.

1314.   Toměi, Wolf von. "Joseph Farrer, ein Schulkamerad
         Zwinglis." NZZ, 1969. Nr. 685.

1315.   Tournier, Camille. La Justification d'après
         Zwingle. Strasbourg: Berger-Levrault, 1853.
         [Strasbourg thesis]

1316.   Towns, Elmer. "Ulrich Zwingli." The Christian
         Hall of Fame. Grand Rapids, Mich.: Baker
         Book House, 1971. 42-43.

1317.   Trog, Hans. "Zwingliausstellung." NZZ,
         1919. Nr. 627.

1318.   _____. "Ein Zwinglibild." NZZ, 1919. Nr. 9.

1319.   _____. "Ein Zwingliporträt (O. Baumbergers)."
         NZZ, 1919. Nr. 829.

1320. Truog, Jakob R. *Ulrich Zwinglis Leben und Werk*. Chur, 1916.

1321. Uhler, Conrad. *Das stemerne Kreuz*. Frauenfeld, 1909. [*]

1322. Ulbach, E. "Ulrich Zwingli." *Bibliotheca Sacra*, 93, 1936, 456-472; 94, 1937, 51-64.

1323. "Ulrich Zwingli gegen den fremden Herrendienst." *Der Protestant*, 1914. Nrs. 20, 21.

#1324. *Ulrich Zwingli. Zum Gedächtnis der Zürcher Reformation 1519-1919*. Zurich: Berichthaus, 1919.
   R: NZZ, 1919. Nr. 327; H. Escher, NZZ, 1919. Nr. 51; Maria Waser, *Die Schweiz*, 1919, pp. 203 ff.

1325. "Ein ungedrucktes Lied über Zwingli. Mitgeteilt von Dr. Wilhelm Josef Meyer." ZWA, 2, 14, 1911, 441-444.

1326. Urner-Astholz, Hildegard. "Nachfahren Ulrich Zwinglis in Stein am Rhein." *Steiner Anzeiger*, 1939.

1327. Usteri, Alfred. "Anna Zwingli." *Religiöses Volksblatt*, 28, 1897, pp. 86 ff.

1328. Usteri, J. "Im Unterliegen-Siegen; zu Huldrych Zwinglis Gedenken." *Monatsblatt der evangelischen Gesellschaft des Kantons Zürich*, 1931. Nr. 12. [*]

1329. Vancandard, E. "Ulrich Zwingli (ou Swingli)." *Dictionaire pratique des connaissances religieuses*, 6, 1928, col. 513 ff.

1330. Van den Broek, L. R. "Gottes Wort wirt die Staub all ring dannen blasen; (Zwingli)." *Ons godsdienstig Leven, Hoorn*, 1931. Nr. 40.

#1331. Vasella, Oskar. "Huldrych Zwingli und seine Gegner." ZSKG, 56, 1962, 281-300.

#1332. _____. *Oesterreich und die Bündnispolitik der katholischen Orte 1527-1529*. Freiburg/Schweiz, 1951.

1333. Vasella, Oskar. "Ulrich Zwingli und Michael Gaismair, der Tiroler Bauernführer." SZG, 24, 1944, 388-413.

1334. _____. "Die Ursachen der Reformation in der deutschen Schweiz." SZG, 27, 1947, 401-424.

1335. _____. "Die Wahl Zwinglis als Leutpriester von Glarus." ZSKG, 51, 1957, 27-35.

1336. Vetter, Ferdinand. "Schweizerische Reformations-legenden. I. Zwinglis Herz; II. Zwinglis Tod; Anhang. Zwinglis Waffen." SZG, 3, 1922, 1-105.

1337. Vetter, Theodor. Literarische Beziehungen zwischen England und der Schweiz im Reformations-zeitalter. Gratulationsschrift zum 450-jährigen Jubiläum der Universität Glasgow, verfasst im Auftrag von Rektor und Senat der Universität Zürich. Zürich: Zürcher & Furrer, 1901.

1338. Vincent, John Martin. Switzerland at the beginning of the sixteenth century. Johns Hopkins University Studies in historical and political Science, XXII: 5. Baltimore: The Johns Hopkins Press, 1904.

1339. Vischer, Eberhard. "Der Schweizerische Reformator Ulrich Zwingli." Zum Gedächtnis der Reformation. Basel: Helbing & Lichtenhahn, 1917. 29-60.

1340. Vögeli, Alfred. "Huldrych Zwingli und der Thurgau; Vortrag." Edited by Evangelische Kirchenrat des Kantons Thurgau. Hüttlingen, 1969.

1341. Vogt, G. "Die Neutralitätspolitik Zwinglis." ZWA, 1, 3, 1898, 41-45.

1342. "Volkslehrkurse der Pestalozzigesellschaft. Kurs 1: Ulrich Zwingli und die Reformation in der Schweiz." NZZ, 1919. Nr. 60.

1343. "Vom Zwinglidenkmal in Zürich." NZZ, 1928. Nr. 2163.

1344. "Von unserm Zürcher Reformator." Monatsblatt
       der Evang. Gesellschaft des Kantons Zürich,
       3, 12, 1919.

1345. "Vor 450 Jahren." Kirchenbote für den Kanton
       Zürich, 55, January 1 1969.

1346. Vuilleumier, H. "Une édition française du
       catéchisme mural de Zurich de 1525."
       Revue de théologie et de philosophie, 1900,
       290-296.

1347. W., B. "Zwinglistudien. 1. Zwinglis Entwicklung
       und Eigenart, 2. Zwinglis reformatorische
       Arbeiten." Reformierte Kirchenzeitung,
       18, 1895, pp. 3 ff.

1348. _____. "Zwinglistudien. 3. Zwingli und Luther."
       Reformierte Kirchenzeitung, 19, 1896, pp. 68 ff.

1349. _____. "Zwinglistudien. 4. Zwinglis Beziehungen
       zu Württemberg." Reformierte Kirchenzeitung,
       19, 1896, pp. 83 ff.

1350. Waldburger, August. "Aus Zwinglis Reise nach
       Marburg 1529 zum Religionsgespräch mit Luther."
       Volkskalender für die reformierte Schweiz und
       ihre Diaspora, 1929. Basel: Krebs.

1351. _____. "Der betende Zwingli." Schweiz.
       Protestantenblatt, 1931. Nr. 41.

1352. _____. "Deutsches Reich und Zwingli."
       Deutsches Protestantenblatt, 1931. Nr. 40.

#1353. _____. Der falsche und der wahre Zwingli.
       Basel: Brodbeck, 1932.
         R: W. Köhler, Basler Nachrichten, 1932. Nr.
         291; L. von Muralt, ZWA, 6, 3, 1935, 188.

1354. _____. "Das gerettete Panner; nach d. Quellen
       erzählt. Von Sebaldus Eremita [pseud. for
       A. Waldburger]." Volkskalender für die
       reformierte Schweiz, 1932.

1355. _____. "En grappige portretten-mystifikatie
       en een ondeskundig bijschrift." Ons
       godsdienstig Leven, Hoorn, 1931. Nr. 978.

1356.   Waldburger, August. "Huldreich Zwingli."
         [Deutsches] Protestantenblatt, 1919. Nr. 3.

1357.   _____. "Huldrich Zwingli en het buitenland."
         Ons godsdienstig Leven, Hoorn, 1931. Nr. 968.

1358.   _____. "Kirch und Politik." Basler Nachrichten,
         1931. Nr. 320.

1359.   _____. "Schweizerische, zürcherische Reformation."
         Schweizerische Theologische Zeitschrift, 1919.
         pp. 15 ff.

1360.   _____. "Der viergeteilte Zwingli." Schweiz.
         Protestantenblatt, 1931. Nrs. 46-49.

1361.   _____. "400 Jahre Zürcher Reformation."
         Protestantische Monatshefte, 1919, 1/2,
         pp. 1 ff.

1362.   _____. "Zwingli." Die Religion in Geschichte
         und Gegenwart, 5, 2250-2260.
             R: W. Köhler, ZWA, 3, 6, 1915, 194-195.

1363.   _____. "Zwingli, der Eidgenosse." Schweizerisches
         Protestantenblatt, 1931. Nr. 38.

1364.   _____. "Zwingli im Krieg." Schweizerisches
         Protestantenblatt, 1931. Nrs. 50-52.

1365.   _____. "Zwingli im letzten Lebensjahr."
         Schweizerisches Protestantenblatt, 1931.
         Nrs. 15, 21, 25-31, 40.

1366.   _____. "Zwingli in seinem Todesjahr."
         Schweizerisches Protestantenblatt, 1931.
         Nr. 10, 17.

1367.   _____. "Zwingli und wir." Sonntagsbeilage
         der National-Zeitung, 1931. Nr. 470.

#1368.   _____. Zwinglis Reise nach Marburg zum Gespräch
         mit Luther 1529. Zurich: Beer, 1929.
             R: W. Kohler, Zeitschrift für die Geschichte
         des Oberrheins, 1930. Nr. 43; W. Köhler,
         Theologische Rundschau, 1932. Nr. 4; L. von
         Muralt, ZWA, 5, 7, 1932, 343.

1369. Waldburger, August. "Zwinglis soziale Sorgen."
       Heimkalender für 1908.

1370. _____. "Zwinglis Tod." Deutsches Protestanten-
       blatt, 1931. Nr. 40.

1371. Waldenmaier, Hermann. "Ulrich Zwingli; zu
       s. 400. Todestag." Geist und Arbeit: deutsche
       evangelische Zeitschrift, 1931. N.F. Nr. 2.

1372. Walter, Anton. Zwingli oder die Schlacht bei
       Kappel. Budapest, 1878. [*]

1373. Walther, Andreas. "Zwinglis Pestlied. Ein
       Beitrag zur Dogmengeschichte der Reformations-
       zeit." Neue kirchliche Zeitschrift, 12, 1901,
       pp. 813 ff.

1374. Walther, Wilhelm. "Reformierte Taktik im
       Sakramentstreit der Reformationszeit."
       Neue kirchliche Zeitschrift, 7, 1896,
       pp. 794 ff., 917 ff.

#1375. Walton, Robert C. "Was there a Turning Point
       of the Zwinglian Reformation?" MQR, 42,
       January 1968, 45-56.

1376. _____. "Zwingli and the Anglo-Saxon World."
       Reformed and Presbyterian World, 30, 5,
       March 1969, 214-218.

#1377. _____. Zwingli's Theocracy. Toronto:
       University of Toronto Press, 1968.
          R: H. W. Pipkin, JCS, 12, 1, 1970,
       147-149; Hans Hillerbrand, Journal
       of the American Academy of Religion,
       36, 1968, 271; Charles Garside, Archiv,
       60, 1, 1969, 130-131; Franklin Littel,
       MQR, 43, 1969, 339-340; M. Haas, ZWA,
       13, 3, 1970, 214-217; See Theodor
       Schlatter.

1378. Wanner, Hans. "Zu Zwinglis Psalmen-
       übersetzung." ZWA, 13, 4, 1970,
       231-233.

1379. Watt, Hugh. "Zwingli." Encyclopaedia of Religion
and Ethics. Edited by James Hastings. Vol.
12. Charles Scribner's Sons, 1955. 873-876.

1380. _____. "Zwingli und Luther." Erasmus, 10, 1957,
272-274.

1381. Weber, Heinrich. "Zwingli ruft auf. 11. Okt.
1882." Letzter Gruss an seine Freunde. Zurich,
1900. pp. 23 ff. [*]

1382. Weber, Walter. "Die Datierung von Zwinglis
Schrift 'Was Zürich und Bern not ze betrachten
sye in dem funförtischen handel'." ZWA,
12, 3, 1965, 222-233.

1383. Weder, Julius. Zwingli als politischer
Reformator, 1882.

1384. Wegeli, R. "Aus der Zürcher Seckelmeisterrechnung
1531." ZWA, 2, 6, 1907, 192.

1385. Wegmann, Hans. "De wedergeboorte van het
Christendom." Ons godsdienstig Leven, Hoorn,
1931. Nr. 40.

1386. _____. "Hoe wij Zwingli zien." Ons godsdienstig
Leven, Hoorn, 1931. Nr. 40.

1387. _____. "War Zwingli Reformator?" Schweizerisches
Protestantenblatt, 1931. Nr. 41.

1388. Wehrlin, Robert. "Zwingli. Zum 400 jährigen
Gedenktag des Beginns seines Zürcher Wirkens."
N. Winterthurer Tagblatt, 1919. Nr. 3.

1389. Weidenmann, Paul. "Zwingli predigt in Zürich
und was seine Zeitgenossen dazu sagen."
Evangelischer Kirchenbote für das Rheintal,
1919. Nr. 1.

1390. _____. "Zwinglis Bedeutung für die Gegenwart."
Evangelischer Kirchenbote für das Rheintal,
1919. Nr. 1.

1391. Weinel, H. "Zwingli-Kontroverse mit Hans Baur."
Die freie Volkskirche, 1931. Nr. 19.

1392. Weisz, Leo. "Das Gefecht am Gubel." NZZ, 1931.
       Nr. 2000.

1393. _____. "Die Geschichte der Kappelerkriege
       nach Hans Edlibach." ZSKG, 1932, 2/3.

1394. _____. "Johannes Stumpfs Geschichte des
       Abendmahlsstreites." ZWA, 5, 4, 1930, 193-221.

1395. _____. "Kritische Bemerkungen zur Historiographie
       der Kappelerkriege." NZZ, 1931. Nr. 132.

1396. _____. "Leo Jud in Einsiedeln." ZWA, 7,
       1943, 409-431, 473-494.

1397. _____. Leo Jud, Ulrich Zwinglis Kampfgenosse
       (1482-1542).Zwingli Bücherei, XXVII. Zurich,
       1942.
           R: L. von Muralt, ZWA, 7, 10, 1943, 640-641.

1398. _____. Nach der Schlacht von Kappel. Zurich:
       Beer, 1937.
           R: L. von Muralt, ZWA, 7, 8, 1942, 533.

#1399. _____. "Die neuere Zwingli-Literatur in
       Ungarn." ZWA, 6, 5, 1936, 282-285.

1400. _____. "Quellen zur Reformationsgeschichte des
       Grossmünsters in Zürich."ZWA, 7, 2, 1939,
       65-90; 3, 1940, 172-202.

1401. _____. "Quellenkunde des zweiten Kappeler-
       krieges." NZZ, 1931. Nr. 1954.

1402. _____. "Ritter Melchior Lussy über Zwinglis
       Tod." ZWA, 4, 13, 1927, 401-407.

1403. _____. "Die Schlacht bei Kappel." NZZ, 1931.
       Nr. 1925.

1404. _____. "Ulrich Dänzlers Lohn." Anzeiger v.
       Uster, 1931. Nr. 236.

1405. _____. "Unbekannte ausländische Quellen zur
       Geschichte der Kappelerkriege." Geschichts-
       freund, 86, 1932.

1406. _____. "Zürich nach Kappel." NZZ, 1931. Nr. 2102.

1407. Weisz, Leo. "Zürich und der evangelische Glaube
in Ungarn." Reformatio, 5, 1956, 639-642.

1408. Wendel, Hermann. "Ulrich Zwingli; zu s. 400.
Todestag." Volksrecht, 1931. Nr. 237.
Vorwärts, October 13, 1931; Arbeiterzeitung,
Wien, October 14, 1931.

1409. Wendorf, Hermann. "Zwinglis Stellung zum Staate."
Staat und Persönlichkeit. Erich Brandenburg
zum 60. Geburtstag. Leipzig: Dieterich'sche
Verlagsbuchandlung, 1928. 91-106.

1410. Werner, August. "Huldreich Zwingli, der Reformator
von Zürich." Helden der christlichen Kirche,
1904, 184-194.

1411. Werner, Martin. "Die Bedeutung Zwinglis für
den Aufbau einer modernen Dogmatik."
Schweizerische theologische Umschau, 1931.
Nr. 7.

1412. _____. "Luthers Urteil über Zwingli."
Schweizerisches reformiertes Volksblatt,
1931. Nr. 41.

1413. Wernle, Paul. "Das angebliche Zürcher
Ratsmandat evangelischer Predigt von 1520."
ZWA, 2, 6, 1907, 166-172.

1414. _____. Der evangelische Glaube nach den
Hauptschriften der Reformatoren: II. Ulrich
Zwingli. Tübingen: Mohr, 1918.
R: W. Köhler, NZZ, 1919. Nrs. 477, 483;
W. Köhler, Theologische Rundschau, N.F. 4,
1932.

1415. _____. "Reformatorisches Glauben und Denken,
5. Zwingli." Kirchenblatt für die reformierte
Schweiz, 20, 1905, 38-42.

#1416. _____. Das Verhältnis der schweizerischen
zur deutschen Reformation. Basel: Helbing
& Lichtenhahn, 1918. See also: Basler Zeitschrift für Geschichte und Altertumskunde,
17, 2, 1918, 226-315.

1417. Wernle, P. "Zu Zwingli und Erasmus." ZWA, 1,
        17, 1904, 470.

1418. _____. "Zum Thema: Zwingli und die Gegenwart."
        Kirchenblatt für die reformierte Schweiz,
        1919, pp. 33 ff.

1419. _____. "Zwinglis und Calvins Stellung zum
        Staat." Verhandlungen des Pfarrvereins des
        Kantons Zürich. Zurich, 1916.

1420. Westermaier. "Das Leben von Huldreich Zwingli
        und Joh. Calvin." Geschichte der Christlichen
        Kirche. Halle, 1846. pp. 1 ff.

1421. Westmijse, G. "Toen de tijden rijpten: Ulrich
        Zwingli, gest. 11. Oct. 1531." Ons
        godsdienstig Leven, Hoorn, 1931. Nr. 40.

1422. Wetli, Karl. "Als ich unerwartet auf meinem
        Zimmer den Gipsabguss von Zwinglis Brustbild
        an der Horgnerkanzel vorfand." 1891.
        Manuscript in possession of Karl Wetli, Obermeilen.
        [*]

1423. _____. "Reformatorenlied zu den in Holz
        geschnitzten Bildern der Reformatoren in
        Horgen." Manuscript in possession of Karl
        Wetli, Obermeilen. [*]

1424. _____. "Vor Nathers Entwurf zum Zwinglidenkmal
        1882." Manuscript in possession of Karl
        Wetli, Obermeilen. [*]

1425. _____. "Das Zwinglidenkmal. Am Tage seiner
        Einweihung, 25. August 1885." Allgemeine
        Schweizer Zeitung. Also: Nachrichten vom
        Zürichsee, September 1, 1885. See also:
        Erinnerungsblätter zur Einweihungsfeier des
        Zwingli-Denkmals in Zürich, 1885, 2, 40/41.
        [*]

#1426. Whitney, James Pounder. "The Helvetic Reformation."
        Cambridge Modern History. Vol II. The Reformation.
        Cambridge: Cambridge University Press, 1903.
        305-341.

1427. Widmer, Sigmund. "Zwinglis Schrift: 'Was Zürich
        und Bern not ze betrachten sye im fünförtigen
        handel'." ZWA, 8, 9, 1948, 535-555.

1428.   "Wie Zwingli predigte." Kirchenbote für die
        evangelisch-reformierten Kirchen Basel-Stadt,
        Glarus, Schaffhausen und der Diaspora der
        Zentralschweiz und im Kanton Solothurn,
        1969. Nr. 1.

1429.   "Ein wiedergefundenes Zwingli-Bildnis."
        NZZ, 1948. Nrs. 2208. 2116.

1430.   Wild, Helen. "Sachregister zu der Gesamtausgabe
        der Werke Zwinglis." ZWA, 8, 1, 1944,
        62-63.

1431.   Wild, H. "Das Zwinglibild." NZZ, 1919.
        Nr. 748.

1432.   _____. "Das Zwinglihaus." NZZ, 1919. Nr. 797.

1433.   Wipf, E. "Huldreich Zwingli." Evang. Gemeinde-
        blatt für Schweizerische Diasporagemeinden,
        1918/1919, Nr. 7.

1434.   Wipf, Jacob. "Zwinglis Beziehungen zu Schaff-
        hausen." ZWA, 5, 1, 1929, 11-41.

1435.   Wirz, Hans Georg. "Ein Dank an Huldrych Zwingli
        zu seinem 400. Todestag." N. Berner Zeitung,
        1931. Nr. 237.

1436.   _____. "Hans Hallers letzter Gang v. Bülach
        nach Kappel. am 10. und 11. Okt. 1531."
        N. Berner Zeitung, 1931. Nr. 237.

1437.   _____. "Huldrych Zwingli." ZWA, 4, 1927,
        413.

1438.   _____. "Huldrych Zwingli." Berner Illustrierte,
        1931. Nr. 41. Supplement to N. Berner Zeitung.

1439.   _____. "Zürcher Familienschicksale im Zeitalter
        Zwinglis." ZWA, 6, 4, 1935, 194-222; 5, 1936,
        242-271; 9, 1938, 470-499; 10, 1938, 537-574.

1440.   _____. "Zwingli." Anzeiger v. Uster, 1931. Nr.
        236. [*]

1441.   Wirz, Paul. "1531-1931; eine Neujahrsbetrachtung."
        Kirchenbote für den Kanton Zürich, 1931. Nr. 1.

#1442. Wolf, Erik. "Die Sozialtheologie Zwinglis."
        <u>Festschrift Guido Kisch, Rechts-historische</u>
        <u>Forschungen</u>. Stuttgart: Kohlhammer,
        1955, 167-188.

 1443. Wolf, Gustav. "Zwingli." <u>Quellenkunde der</u>
        <u>deutschen Reformationsgeschichte</u>. Vol. II.
        Gotha: F. A. Perthes, 1916.

 1444. Wolfer, Albert. "Von Zwinglis Glauben,
        Streben und Wirken." <u>Religiöses Volksblatt</u>,
        62. Nrs. 41-44.

 1445. Wolfer, Theodor Muller. <u>Le siècle du schisme</u>
        <u>religieux</u>. Bern, 1925. 5-54.

 1446. "Woran denken Sie, wenn Sie an Zwingli denken?"
        <u>Kirchenbote für den Kanton Zürich</u>, 55,
        January 1, 1969, 4.

 1447. "Worte Zwinglis über Luther." <u>Schweizerisches</u>
        <u>Protestantenblatt</u>, 6, 52, December 29, 1883,
        430-431.

#1448. Wuhrmann, Willy. "Bibliographie des Zürcher
        Reformationsjubiläums 1919." ZWA, 3, 15,
        1920, 477-486.

 1449. _____. "Huldreich Zwingli." <u>Der Kinder Sonntag</u>,
        1919. Nr. 1.

 1450. _____. "Die Zürcher Teilnehmer an der Berner
        Disputation im Januar 1528." ZWA, 2, 15,
        1912, 451-455.

 1451. _____. "Zwei Namensvettern als Zwinglis
        Helfer am Grossmünster." ZWA, 3, 5, 1915,
        148-153.

 1452. _____. "Die Zwingliausstellung in Zürich."
        <u>Schweizerisches Protestantenblatt</u>, 1919.
        pp. 165 ff.

 1453. _____. "Zwinglis Amtsantritt in Zürich."
        <u>Kirchenbote für den Kanton Zürich</u>, 1919. Nr. 1.

 1454. _____. "Zwinglis beabsichtigte Amtsniederlegung."
        ZWA, 3, 2, 1913, 50-54.

1455. Wuhrmann, Willy. "Zwinglis Bedeutung für die Gegenwart." Schweizerisches Protestantenblatt, 1919. pp. 10 ff.

1456. _____. "Zwinglis Lied." ZWA, 2, 15, 1912, 50-54.

1457. _____. "Zwinglis Werke." Schweizerische Theologische Zeitschrift, 1917. pp. 21 ff.

1458. Wunderli, Gustav. Huldrych Zwingli und die Reformation in Zürich nach den Tagsatzungs- protokollen und Zürcher. Obrigkeitlichen Erlassen. Zurich, 1897.

1459. Wymann, Ed. "Zwingliana." Schweizerische Rundschau, 1904/1905, 6.

#1460. Wyss, Bernhard. Die Chronik des Bernhard Wyss 1519-1530. Quellen zur schweizerischen Reformationsgeschichte, I. Edited by G. Finsler. Basel: Basler Buch- und Antiquariats- Handlung, 1901.

1461. Yoder, J. H. "Evolution of the Zwinglian Reformation." MQR, 43, January 1969, 95-122.

1462. _____. "The Turning Point in the Zwinglian Refor- mation." MQR, 32, April 1958, 128-140.

1463. Zeeuw, P. d. "De schrynwerker van Zürich. Ein verhaal uit het leven van Ulrich Zwingli" Geitl. door Menno. 2nd ed. Delft, Meinema, 1955.

1464. Zehender, Ferdinand. "Anna Zwingli." Hauspoesie. Frauenfeld, 1882. 20-21. [*]

1465. Zeller-Werdmuller, H. "Hans Jakob Stampfers Gedenkmünze auf Ulrich Zwingli." ZWA, 1, 10, 1901, 217-221.

1466. _____. "Zwinglis Waffen." ZWA, 1, 6, 1899, 105-108.

1467. Zemp, Joseph. Die schweizerischen Bilderchroniken und ihre Architectur-Darstellungen. Zurich, 1897. 141-159.

1468.   Zentralbibliothek. Zwingli-Ausstellung. Zurich:
         Berichthaus, 1919.

1469.   Zickendraht, K. "Das Blutwunder in Oberflachs
         vom 26. Juli 1531." ZWA, 3, 4, 1914, 117-
         124.

1470.   Ziegler, Albert. "Aus Huldrych Zwinglis Leben
         und Wirken." Landbote, 1931. Nr. 236.

1471.   _____. "Die Einführung der Reformation in
         Winterthur." Landbote, 1931. Nr. 236.

1472.   Zimmermann, Arnold. "1531--11. Okt.--1931."
         Zürcher Post, 1931. Nr. 238.

1473.   _____. "Gastfreundschaft in der Reformation."
         Festgabe Ed. Rübel. Zurich: Schulthess,
         1946. 165-173.

1474.   _____. "Zu Zwinglis Andenken." Kirchenfreund,
         1931. Nr. 42.

1475.   _____. Die Zwingligedenkfeier in Jahre 1931.
         Zurich: Schulthess, 1932.
            R: W. Köhler, Theologische Rundschau, N.F. 4,
         1932.

1476.   Zimmermann, Hans. "Das Vermächtnis eines
         Frühvollendeten." Gemeindeblatt für Gemeinden
         im Kreise Schlüchtern, 1931. Nr. 7/8.

1477.   "Zuinglio (Ulrico)." Enciclopedia Vniversal
         Ilvstrada. Vol. 70. Madrid: Espasa-Calpe,
         S.A., n.d. 1490-1493.

1478.   "Zum 400jährigen Gedächtnis des Amtsantrittes
         von Zwingli in Zürich." Gemeindeblatt für
         die Glieder und Freunde der Grossmünster-
         gemeinde, 1918. Nr. 6.

1479.   "Zur Erinnerung an den Beginn der Zürcher-
         reformation durch Zwinglis Amtsantritt am
         Neujahr 1519." Die Glocke, 27, 4, January
         1919.

1480.   "Zur Zwinglifeier am 5. Januar 1919." Edited by
         the Kirchenrat des Kantons Baselstadt. Basel, 1919.

1481. "Zurich recalls Zwingli." Christianity Today,
      13, January 17, 1969, 42.

1482. "Zwei Ausstellungen." NZZ, 1919. Nr. 261.

1483. "Zwei Disticha des Esslinger Schulmeisters Ägidius
      Krautwasser (Lympholerius) auf den Tod
      Zwinglis." ZWA, 2, 9, 1909, 278-279.[*]

1484. "Der Zweite Landfriede vom 15. Nov. 1531."
      N. Winterthurer Tagblatt, 1931. Nr. 271

1485. "Zwingle ou Zwingli (Ulric)." Nouveau Larousse
      Illustré Dictionnaire Universel Encyclopédique.
      Vol. 7. Paris: Librairie Larousse, 1933. 1431.

1486. "Zwingle ou Zwingli (Ulrich)." Larousse du
      XXe Siècle. Vol. 6. Paris: Librairie Larousse,
      1933. 1145.

1487. "Zwingli." Pamphlet edited by a circle of Zurich
      pastors. Zurich: Schaufelberger, 1919.

1488. "Zwingli als Seelsorger." Kirchliches Gemeinde-
      blatt für die evangelische Kirchgemeinde
      Horgen, 3, 1.

1489. "Zwingli. Christliche Stimmen." Mitteilungen
      der Schweizer Gruppe für Freundschaftsarbeit
      der Kirchen, 1919. Nr. 7.

1490. "Zwingli et les blocus alimentaires." Semaine
      religieuse, 1919. Nr. 3.

1491. "Zwingli führt in Zürich die Reformation durch."
      Der Protestant, 1918. Nr. 23.

1492. "Zwingli, Huldreich." [Deutsches] Protestanten-
      blatt, 1919. Nr. 2.

1493. "Zwingli, Huldreich." The New Schaff-Herzog
      Encyclopedia of Religious Knowledge. Edited by
      Samuel M. Jackson. Vol. 12. Grand Rapids,
      Michigan: Baker Book House, 1953. 538-546.

1494. "Zwingli, Huldreich or Ulrich.' The Columbia
      Encyclopedia. 3rd ed. New York: Columbia
      University Press, 1963. 2387-2388.

1495. "Zwingli, Huldreich or Ulrich." The Columbia-
Viking Desk Encyclopedia. 3rd ed. New York:
The Viking Press, 1968. 1202.

1496. "Zwingli, Huldrych." Volksrecht, 1919. Nr. 2;
Arbeiterzeitung, 1919. Nr. 2.

1497. "Zwingli, Huldrych in Glarus 1506-1516." By
A. D. Tages-Anzeiger, 1952. Nr. 253.

1498. "Zwingli im Kampf gegen die Volksfeinde."
Baselbieter Kirchenbote, 1918. Nr. 7.

1499. "Zwingli in Glarus und Einsiedeln." Der
Protestant, 1918. Nr. 21.

1500. "Zwingli in Zürich 1519-1522." Der Protestant,
1918. Nr. 22.

1501. "Zwingli sco hom da stadi; sül anniv. da sia
mort als 11 Oct. 1531." Fögl d'Engiadina,
1931. Nr. 80.

1502. "Zwingli, Ulrich." Compton's Pictured Encyclopedia and Fact Finder. Vol. 24.
Chicago: F. E. Compton Co., 1968. 370.

1503. "Zwingli, Ulrich als Politiker." Volksstimme,
Sozialdemokratisches Tagblatt für die Stadt
St. Gallen und die Kantone St. Gallen,
Appenzell und Glarus, 1919. Nr. 5.

1504. "Zwingli, Ulrich or Huldreich." The New
International Encyclopaedia. Vol. 23.
New York: Dodd, Mead and Co., 1935.
886-887.

1505. "Zwingli, Ulrich (or Huldreich)." The Oxford
Dictionary of the Christian Church. Edited by
F. L. Cross. London: Oxford University
Press, 1957. 1491-1492.

1506. "Zwingli (Ulrich ou Huldrych)." Grand Larousse
Encyclopédique. Vol. 10. Paris: Libraire
Larousse, 1964. 1031.

1507. "Zwingli, Ulrich, und die zürcherische Armenpflege." Der Armenpfleger, Monatsschrift
für Armenpflege und Jugendfürsorge, 1919. Nr. 5.

1508. "Zwingli und Bern." Der Säemann, Monatsblatt
       der bernischen Landeskirche, 1919. Nr. 2.

1509. "Zwingli und die Gegenwart." Baselbieter
       Kirchenbote, 1919. Nr. 2.

1510. "Zwingli und die Kirche." By F. G. Volkszeitung
       d. Bez. Pfäffikon, 1931. Nr. 122.

1511. "Zwingli und die Schule." Schweizerische
       Lehrerzeitung, 1919. Nr. 1.

1512. "Zwingli und die zürcherische Kunst zur Zeit
       der Reformation." NZZ, 1918. Nr. 1617.

1513. "Zwingli, ein zweiter Niklaus von der Flüe,
       der auch wohl würdig wäre, dass sein
       Vierhundertjahrgedächtnis von allen Glocken
       der Eidgenossenschaft gefeiert würde."
       Der Protestant, 1918. Nr. 25.

1514. "Zwingli-Ausstellung." NZZ, 1919. Nr. 624.

1515. "Zwingli-Ausstellung." NZZ, 1919. Nr. 888.

1516. Zwingli Ausstellung [Katalog]. Zurich: Zentral-
       bibliothek, 1919.

1517. "Zwingli-Ausstellung in der Zentralbibliothek
       Zürich." NZZ, 1931. Nr. 1938; Zürcher
       Post, 1931. Nr. 234, 235.

1518. "Das Zwingli-Bild von Emil Egli bis Fritz
       Blanke." NZZ, 1969. Nr. 4.

1519. "Zwingli -- Christ und Staatsmann; zum Beginn
       der Zürcher Reformation." Der Landbote,
       1969. Nr. 15.

1520. "Das Zwinglidenkmal auf dem Schlachtfeld von
       Kappel." ZWA, 2, 14, 1911, 433-434.

1521. "Zwingli-Denkmal. Erinnerungsblätter mit
       Illustrationen." Zurich: Zürcher & Furrer, n.d.

1522. "Die Zwinglihütte." Der Protestant, 1, 1898,
       pp. 43 ff.

1523. "Zwingli-Kantate." Composed by Gustav Weber;
Text by Conrad Ferdinand Meyer; Arranged for
church choir by Hans Huldreich Baur. Der
Volkskalender für die reformierte Schweiz
und ihre Diaspora 1932. Basel: Krebs, 1932.[*]

1524. "Zwingli-Lithographie von Ernst Georg Rüegg."
NZZ, 1931. Nr. 1925; Kirchgem.-blatt von
Neumünster, 1931. Nr. 12.

1525. "Zwinglimedaille." NZZ, 1919. Nr. 841.

1526. "Eine Zwingli-Medaille." NZZ, 1919. Nr. 455.

1527. "Zwinglis Bedeutung für die Gegenwart."
Zürcher Post, 1919. Nr. 2.

1528. "Zwinglis Bildnis in der schweizerischen
Medaillenkunst." NZZ, 1923. Nr. 1587.

1529. "Zwinglis Feldzugsplan vom Jahre 1524."
Der Protestant, 1914. Nr. 22.

1530. "Zwinglis Kindheit, Knaben- und Studentenzeit."
Der Protestant, 1918. Nr. 20.

1531. "Zwinglis letzte Lebensjahre und Ende."
Der Protestant, 1919. Nr. 4.

1532. "Zwinglis letzte Worte." Der Protestant, 1919.
Nr. 5.

1533. "Zwinglis Sprache." Der Protestant, 1919. Nr. 1.

1534. "Zwingli's 'A Short and Clear Exposition of the
Christian Faith'." Masterpieces of the
Christian Faith in Summary Form. Edited by
Frank N. Magill and Ian P. McGreal. New
York: Harper & Row, 1963. 363-367.

1535. "Zwinglis Tod; (Aus d. ältesten Lebensbild
Zwinglis v. Oswald Mykonius 1532, a. d. Lat.)."
Anzeiger von Uster, 1931. Nr. 236.

1536. "Zwinglis Waffen." Der Protestant, 1915. Nr. 9.

1537. "Zwingli-Vorträge." NZZ, 1919. Nr. 291.

1538. "Zwingliworte über Krieg und Frieden."
Volkskalender für die reformierte Schweiz und
ihre Diaspora 1936. Basel: Krebs, 1936.

II. Zwingli Sources

A. Collected Works, including Anthologies

#1539. Bromiley, G. W. (ed.). Zwingli and Bullinger.
Library of Christian Classics, XXIV.
Philadelphia: Westminster Press, 1953.
R: O. Chadwick, JTS, 5, April 1954,
102-104; C. S. Malefyt, Westminster
Theological Journal, 16, November 1953,
122-124; F. E. Mayer, Concordia Theological
Monthly, 25, 1954, 247-248; E. T. Thompson,
8, July 1954, 357-358; T. D. Price,
Review and Expositor, 50, October 1953, 520;
Wilhelm Pauck, Union Seminary Quarterly
Review, 9, January 1954, 50-52.

#1540. Farner, Oskar (ed.). Aus Zwinglis Predigten zu
den Evangelien Matthäus, Markus, und Johannes.
Veröffentlichungen der Rosa-Ritter-Zweifel-
Stiftung, religiöse Reihe. Zurich: Berichthaus,
1957.
R: L. von Muralt, ZWA, 10, 8, 1957, 473-
487.

#1541. _____. Aus Zwinglis Predigten zu Jesaja und
Jeremia. Veröffentlichungen der Rosa-Ritter-
Zweifel-Stiftung, Religiöse Reihe. Zurich:
Berichthaus, 1957.
R: L. von Muralt, ZWA, 10, 8, 1957,
473-487; Joachim Heubach, ThL, 85, 1960,
292; P. Sherding, Revue d'histoire et
de philosophie religieuses, 37, 1957,
377-378.

1542. _____. Gott ist Meister, Zwingli-Worte für
unsere Zeit. Zurich: Zwingli Verlag,
1944.
R: L. von Muralt, ZWA, 7, 10, 1943, 635.

#1543. _____. Huldrych Zwinglis Briefe. 2 vols.
Zurich, 1918, 1920.
R: W. Köhler, ZWA, 3, 16, 1920, 529.

1544. Graf, Chr. Zwingli-Abschnitte aus seinen
Schriften. Zurich: Füssli,1917.
R: Gerold M. von Knonau, ZWA, 3, 10,
1917, 322-323; W. Köhler, Theologische
Rundschau, 20, 1917; ThL, 42, 1917, 412.

#1545. Hillerbrand, Hans J. The Reformation. A
Narrative History Related by Contemporary
Observers and Participants. New York:
Harper & Row, 1964.
R: L. Spitz, JCH, 34, 4, 462.

#1546. Huldreich Zwinglis sämtliche Werke. 14 vols.
Corpus Reformatorum. Vols 88 ff. Edited by
Emil Egli, G. Finsler et al. Leipzig, Berlin:
Schwetschke & Sohn, 1905 ff. Also: Zurich,
Berichthaus.

#1547. Jackson, Samuel M. The Latin Works of Huldreich
Zwingli. 3 vols. Philadelphia: The Heidelberg
Press, 1912, 1922, 1929.
R: W. Köhler, ZWA, 4, 13, 1927, 412-413.

#1548. _____. Selected Works of Huldreich Zwingli.
Philadelphia: University of Pennsylvania
Press, 1901.
R: W. Köhler, ThL, 27, 1902, 403.

#1549. Kidd, Beresford James. Documents Illustrative
of the Continental Reformation. Oxford:
Clarendon Press, 1911.
R: W. Köhler, HZ, 108, 1912.

#1550. Köhler, Walther. Das Buch der Reformation.
Munich: Reinhardt, 1926.

#1551. Künzli, Edwin. Huldrych Zwingli: Auswahl seiner
Schriften. Zurich: Zwingli Verlag, 1962.
R: H. Gutzwiller, ZSKG, 57, 1963, 85-87;
G. Locher, HZ, 203, 1966, 759-760;
C. Bonorand, ThZ, 20, 1964, 148.

#1552. Lau, Franz (ed.). Der Glaube der Reformatoren:
Luther, Zwingli, Calvin. Bremen: Carl
Schünemann, 1964.

1553. Manschreck, Clyde L. A History of Christianity:
Readings in the History of the Church from
the Reformation to the Present. Englewood
Cliffs, N.J.: Prentice-Hall, 1965. 64-74.

135

#1554. Schmidt-Clausing, Fritz. <u>Zwinglis liturgische Formulare</u>. Frankfurt am Main: Otto Lembeck, 1970.

#1555. <u>Ulrich Zwingli. Eine Auswahl aus seinen Schriften</u>. Edited and selected by G. Finsler, W. Köhler and Arnold Ruegg. Zurich: Schulthess & Co., 1918.

1556. "Worte Zwinglis über Luther." <u>Schweizerisches Protestantenblatt</u>, 6, 52, 1883, 430-431.

1557. Wuhrmann, Willy. "Eine Auswahl aus Zwinglis Schriften." I: 1918, 237 ff; II: 280 ff.; III: 340 ff., 348 ff.; IV: 1919, 115 ff.

#1558. <u>Zwinglis Hauptschriften</u>. Vols. 1, 2, 3, 4, 7, 9, 10, 11. Edited by Fritz Blanke, Oskar Farner, Oskar Frei and Rudolf Pfister. Zurich: Zwingli Verlag, 1940 ff.
    R: L. von Muralt, ZWA, 7, 10, 1943, 631-635; ZWA, 10, 2, 1954, 141-143; T. F. Torrance, SJT, 1949, 441-444; O. Vasella, ZSKG, 58, 1964, 148-150; C. G. Krodel, JCH, 33, December 1964, 496.

136

B.   Individual Writings

1559.   Altherr, A.   "Aus Zwinglis Briefen."
        Schweizerisches Protestantenblatt, 6, 52, 1883,
        433-437.

#1560. Battles, Ford Lewis (ed.).   Huldreich Zwingli.
        A Comparative Essay on Forms of Government.
        Pittsburgh, Pa.: Pittsburgh Theological
        Seminary, 1970.   See Nr. 1594.

1561.   _____. (trans.) "Enthusiasm for Erasmus."
        Hartford Quarterly, 5, 4, Summer 1965, 67-68.

1562.   Bruppacher, Heinrich (trans.). "Leitstern,
        Zwinglis; Brief Zwinglis." Evangelisches
        Wochenblatt, 1904. Nr. 42.

1563.   Cochrane, Arthur C. "Zwingli's Sixty-seven
        Articles of 1523." Reformed Confessions of
        the 16th Century. Philadelphia: The
        Westminster Press, 1966. 33-44.

#1564. Courvoisier, Jacques (trans.). Brève instruction
        chrétienne, 1523. Les cahiers du renouveau, IX.
        Geneva, 1953.

1565.   Egli, Emil. "Ein Autograph Zwinglis und ein
        Brief Leo Juds." ZWA, 1, 10, 1901, 222-223.

1566.   _____. "Vorarbeiten für eine Neuausgabe
        der Zwinglischen Werke. 1. Zwingli an den
        Rat zu Konstanz, 5. August 1523." ZWA, 1,
        1, 1897, 8-11.

1567.   _____. "Vorarbeiten für eine Neuausgabe
        der Zwinglischen Werke. 8. Ex disputatione
        Bernensi." ZWA, 1, 6, 1899, 111.

1568.   _____. "Vorarbeiten für eine Neuausgabe der
        Zwinglischen Werke. 9. De moderatione et
        sua vitate. . . ." ZWA, 1, 6, 1899, 111.

1569.   _____. "Vorarbeiten zu einer Neuausgabe
        der Zwinglischen Werke. 16. Zwingli an Jacob
        Werdmüller, 24. Juni 1529." ZWA, 1, 7,
        1900, 132-133.

1570. "Einige Anweisungen wie man edle junge Leute erziehen soll." Evangelisches Schulblatt, 104, 1, 1969, 1.

1571. Farner, Oskar. "Ein unveröffentlicher Brief Zwinglis." ZWA, 9, 4, 1950, 247-248.

1572. _____. "Zwingliworte." Zwingli-Kalender 1938. Basel: Reinhardt, 1938.

1573. Forster, Leonard (ed.). "Gebetslied in der Pest." The Penguin Book of German Verse. Baltimore: Penguin Books, 1966. 67-70.

1574. Fosdick, Harry Emerson (ed.). "From An Account of the Faith." Great Voices of the Reformation: An Anthology. New York: Random House, 1952. 179-192.

1575. _____. "From On True and False Religion." Great Voices of the Reformation: An Anthology. New York: Random House, 1952. 161-178.

1576. Goeters, J. F. Gerhard. "Ein Auszug aus Zwinglis 'In Catabaptistarum strophas elenchus' als antitäuferisches Flugblatt." ThZ, 9, 1953, 395-397.

1577. Hillerbrand, Hans J. (ed.). "Huldrych Zwingli: Commentary on True and False Religion 1525." The Protestant Reformation. New York: Harper & Row, 1968. 108-121.

#1578. Huldrych Zwingli: Von göttlicher und menschlicher Gerechtigkeit. Selected and introduced by Leonhard von Muralt and Oskar Farner. Zurich, Rascher, 1934.
    R: H. Escher, ZWA, 6, 1, 1934, 61; W. Köhler, HZ, 150, 1934.

1579. Jeschke, J. G. Počet z víry a výklad víry. Dva vyznavačske listy curyšského reformátora. Praha; Kalich, 1953
    R: Rudolf Pfister, ZWA, 10, 1, 1954, 62-63.

1580. "On Mercenary Soldiers." The World's Famous Orations. Edited by William Jennings Bryan. Vol. 7. New York: Funk & Wagnalls Co., 1906. 30-37. Also: 20 Centuries of Great Preaching. Vol. 2. Waco, Texas: Word Books, 1971. 124-128.

1581. Mesnard, P. "La pédagogie évangélique de Zwingli." Revue Thomiste, 1953, 367-386.

1582. Meyer, Carl S. Luther's and Zwingli's Propositions for Debate; The Ninety-Five Theses of 31 October 1517 and the Sixty-Seven Articles of 19 January 1523. Leiden: E. J Brill, 1963.
R: Lewis W. Spitz, Concordia Theological Monthly, 36, 1965, 187.

1583. "Ein missive, von einem frommen eidgnossen zu sinem frund geschriben, innhaltend ein sümm einer predig, die ietz kürzlich zu Zürich ist beschehen." ZWA, 3, 11, 1918, 339-347.

#1584. Muras, Gerhard Gunther (trans.). Christliche Anleitung. Furche-Bücherei, Nr. 207. Hamburg: Furche Verlag, 1962.

1585. "On the Choice and Free Use of Foods." 20 Centuries of Great Preaching. Edited by Clyde Fant, Jr. and William M. Pinson, Jr. Vol. 2. Waco, Tx.: Word Books, 1971. 96-124.

#1586. Oorthuys, Gerardus (trans.). Huldreich Zwinglis Zeven en Zestig artikelen en Korte christelyke inleiding. Nijkerk, 1913.

1587. Pipkin, H. Wayne (trans.). "Concerning Steadfastness and Perseverance in Goodness." 20 Centuries of Great Preaching. Edited by Clyde Fant, Jr. and William M. Pinson, Jr. Vol. 2. Waco, Tx.: Word Books, 1971. 92-96.

1588. _____. "Zwingli, the laity and the orders; from the cloister into the world." Hartford Quarterly, 8, Winter 1968, 32-41.

#1589. _____. "Zwingli's Short Christian Instruction: An Annotated Translation." Part Two of The Nature and Development of the Zwinglian Reformation to August, 1524. Hartford, 1968. 176-245.

1590. Preble, Henry (trans.). "About the exclusion from the sacrament. Zwingli's advice to the Council at Zurich." Unpublished English translation prepared for Samuel M. Jackson. 4 pages. [This and other Preble manuscripts are located at Union Theological Seminary in New York City.]

1591. Preble, Henry (trans.). "Accounts in Latin of the Marburg Conference." November, 1898.

1592. _____. "The Canon of the Mass, Epichiresis." January, 1900.

1593. _____. "Defence of his pamphlet on the canon of the Mass." 1912.

1594. _____. "First fruits of a commentary on the prophet Isaiah, with an exposition of the author's reasons for his interpretation in the case of all uncertain passages by Huldreich Zwingli." n.d.

1595. _____. "A friendly exegesis or exposition, of the matter of the Eucharist to Martin Luther." October, 1900.

1596. _____. "Huldreich Zwingli to Francis Lambert and all the brethren who are sincere in the faith at Strassburg, preaching or confessing the faith of our Lord Jesus Christ." October, 1901.

1597. _____. "Huldreich Zwingli's prefatory remarks to students of the classic tongues, prefixed to the Coeperinus-Cratander edition of Pindar of the Year 1526, and his letter to the reader attached by way of epilogue to that edition." March 1, 1897.

1598. _____. "Huldreich Zwingli's Reply to a letter of Johann Bugenhagen of Pomerania." January 8, 1901.

1599. _____. "Huldreich Zwingli's reply to letters of Theobald Billicanus and Urbanus Rhegius." February, 1902.

#1600. _____. "A Letter of Huldreich Zwingli to Matthew Alber, Preacher at Reutlingen, on the Lord's Supper." January 8, 1901.

1601. _____. "Questions in regard to the Sacrament of Baptism, put to Huldreich Zwingli by a certain scholar." May, 1900.

1602. Preble, Henry (trans.). "Subsidiary Essay or Crown of the Work on the Eucharist." October, 1901.

1603. _____. "Zwingli to Urbanus Rhegius, grace and peace from the Lord." February 14, 1902.

1604. Reichenbach, A. (trans.). The Christian Education of Youth. Collegeville, Pa.: Thompson Brothers, 1899.

1605. Rüsch, E. G. An den Jungen Mann. Zwingli Bücherei, LXXXII. Zurich: Zwingli Verlag, 1957.

1606. Schmidt-Clausing, Fritz. Zwinglis Kanonversuch. Frankfurt am Main: Otto Lembeck, 1969.

1606a. _____. Zwinglis Zürcher Protokoll. Frankfurt am Main: Otto Lembeck, 1972.
    R: M. Haas, ZWA, 13, 7, 1972, 490.

1607. Scott, W. (ed.). "On the Nature of the Sacraments." Sources of Protestant Theology. New York: Bruce Publishing Co., 1971. 51-58.

1608. Spitta, Friedr. "Chiantzun, una spirituala a ruguar Deis etc. (romanische translation of Zwingli's song, "Herr nun heb den wagen self" etc." Monatsschrift für Gottesdienst und kirchliche Kunst, 3, 1898, 2, 62.

1609. Spitz, Lewis W. (ed.). "Zwingli, The First Disputation and the Sixty-seven Articles." The Protestant Reformation. Englewood Cliffs, N. J.: Prentice-Hall, Inc., 1966. 77-88.

1610. "Tapferkeit." ZWA, 1, 7, 1900, 133.

#1611. Thompson, Bard (ed.). "Action or Use of the Lord's Supper. Easter 1525." Liturgies of the Western Church. New York: The World Publishing Co., 1961. 149-156.

#1612. _____. "Liturgy of the Word 1525." Liturgies of the Western Church. New York: The World Publishing Co., 1961. 147-148.

1613. Troll, Joh. Konrad. "Zwingli an den Rat zu Winterthur. 3 Briefe, dat. 1517.XI.6; 1523.VI.1; 1529.V.16." Zur Geschichte der Stadtkirche zu Winterthur. Neujahrsblatt von der Bürgerbibliothek zu Winterthur, 1844.

1614.   "Ein unveröffentlichter Brief Zwinglis (28. Sept. 1531) mitgeteilt von Wolf von Toměi." NZZ, 1969. Nr. 453.

1615.   Walther, Otto (ed.). Von Freiheit der Speisen. Neudrucke deutscher Litteraturwerke des XVI & XVII Jahrhunderts, CLXXIII. Halle a. S.: Max Niemeyer, 1900.

1616.   Widmer, Sigmund. "Zwinglis Schrift: 'Was Zürich und Bern not ze betrachten sye im fünförtigen Handel'." ZWA, 8, 1948, 535-555.

1617.   "Zwingli an seine Gattin: Brief aus Bern 11 Januar 1528." Der Brief, 1950.

1618.   "Zwingli antwortet einem Täufer: Entwurf zu einer Entgegnung auf die Schrift eines Täufers." Mennonitische Geschichtsblätter, N.F. 19, 14, 1962, 23-27.

1619.   Zwingli, Ulrich and Albertus Burerius. "18 ungedruckte Briefe von Ulrich Zwingli und Albertus Burerius an Beatus Rhenanus. Mitgeteilt von Daniel Albert Fechter." Archiv für schweizerische Geschichte, 10, 1855, 185-211.

Index of Subjects

Drama, 233, 251, 348, 933, 1017, 1022, 1023, 1163, 1372
Dürer, Albrecht, 230, 376, 1166, 1209, see also: Zwingli,
    Portraits of

Early Reformation, 162, 1081, 1115, 1153, 1276, 1303, 1453,
    1500, 1519
Ecclesiology, 215, 218, 438, 486, 565, 1120, 1510
Eck, John, 868
Edlibach, Hans, 522, 691, 1393
Education, 94, 103, 104, 476, 515, 534, 577, 702, 816, 826,
    861, 934, 937, 941, 1041, 1084, 1133, 1143a, 1145, 1238,
    1257, 1511, 1570, 1581, 1604, 1605
Education of Youth, On the, 1570, 1581, 1604, 1605
Einsiedeln, 160, 161, 337, 807, 1279, 1396, 1397, 1499
Elijah, 874
Empire, The, 736, 1018, 1352
Emser, Jerome, 343, 344, 741
England, 323, 1095, 1337, 1376, see also: Anglicanism
English Translations of Zwingli's Works, 1539, 1545, 1547-
    1549, 1553, 1560, 1561, 1574, 1575, 1577, 1580, 1582,
    1585, 1587-1604, 1607, 1609, 1611, 1612
Epistemology, 1304
Epitaphs, 346, 458, 673
Erasmus, Desiderius, 444, 688, 712, 891, 1125, 1417, 1561
Ethics, 487, 608, 825, 1051
Eucharist, see: Lord's Supper
Exposition of the Christian Faith, 602a, 1534, 1579
Exposition of the Sixty-seven Theses, 227, 460, 1045

Fabri, Johann, 607, 617
Faith, 764, 958, 1053
Farel, William, 1064
Farrer, Joseph, 1314
Finances, 198, 505, 661, 662, 1384
Foreign Service, 310, 1323, see also: Mercenaries
Fourth Centennial of Zwingli's Death, 32, 79, 126, 128,
    137, 369, 408, 512, 513, 516, 518, 533, 596, 597,
    655, 683, 694, 839, 840, 843, 907, 913, 936, 952,
    968, 970, 973, 1020, 1022, 1042, 1062, 1132, 1158,
    1175, 1192, 1196, 1219, 1228, 1303, 1371, 1408, 1435,
    1501
France, 781
Francis II, 549
Frederich the Great, 765
Friendly Exegesis of the Eucharist, 1595
Fuchstein, Hans von, 298
Funk, Ulrich, 278

Karlstadt, Andreas, 255, 553, 663
Knonau, Gerold Meyer von, 21, 23, 1099
Krautwasser, Ägidius, 456, 1483
Kurze Christliche Einleitung, 1564, 1584, 1586, 1589
Küsnacht, 225

Labyrinth, 45
Lactantius, 179
Laity, 1085, 1588
Lambert, Francis, 962, 1596
Landeskirche, 988
Law, 14, 341, 622
Lavater, Hans Rudolf, 367
Legends, 140, 883, 1336
Letters of Zwingli, see: Zwingli, Correspondence of
Lisighaus, 256
Liturgy, see: Worship
Lombard, Peter, 460
Lord's Supper, 37, 38, 67, 73, 93, 146, 171, 199, 200,
     205, 540, 560, 618, 663, 669, 779, 782, 783, 785,
     787, 802, 823, 867, 887, 1048, 1118, 1200, 1202,
     1214, 1222, 1251, 1394, 1591-1593, 1595, 1596, 1598-
     1600, 1602, 1603, 1611, 1612
Lucerne, 217
Lussy, Melchior, 1402
Luther, Martin, 29, 44, 82,   92, 98, 153, 185, 362,
     431, 444, 482, 506, 553, 560, 565, 618, 688, 730,
     742, 755, 768, 775, 776, 782, 802, 822, 827, 857,
     858, 867, 878, 885, 897, 898, 939, 988a, 1048, 1100, 1103,
     1124, 1146, 1147, 1184, 1205, 1213, 1220, 1221, 1223,
     1233, 1236, 1264, 1277, 1300, 1348, 1350, 1368, 1380,
     1412, 1447, 1552, 1556, 1595, see also: Friendly
     Exegesis, Marburg
Lutheranism, 770

Magistracy, 486
Man, Knowledge, View of, 224, 1006, 1043
Mandate of 1520, 737, 1413
Marburg, 412, 413, 743, 753, 754, 768, 770, 778, 784, 1201,
     1202, 1236, 1250, 1350, 1368, 1591
Marignano, 1170
Marriage Tribunal, 697, 788, 806
Marti, Paul, 829
Martyrs, 556
Mary, 446, 447, 687, 882, 1300
Mass, The, 343, 344, 819, 1189, 1233
Medicine, 744
Megger, Ulrich, 1469

Index of Reviewers

Moeller, B., 75, 671, 1145
Muralt, L. von, 108, 203, 209, 214, 377, 388, 394, 404,
    412, 419, 431, 494, 588, 651, 723, 743, 879, 882,
    1069, 1121, 1353, 1368, 1397, 1398, 1540, 1541, 1542,
    1558

Nichols, R. H., 1118

Osterhaven, M. E., 1121

Pauck, W., 1539
Pfister, R., 171, 204, 405, 406, 802, 1185, 1186, 1293, 1579
Pipkin, H. W., 1377
Porter, H. C., 1121
Potter, G. R., 1377
Price, T. D., 1539

Reimann, H., 1214
Rich, A., 405
Richards, G. W., 1113
Rieser, E., 606
Rogge, J., 547, 1088
Rowley, H. H., 547
Rüsch, E. G., 407, 530, 676, 1185, 1239

Sasse, H., 1174
Scherding, P., 886, 1174, 1541
Schlatter, T., 1377
Schmid, W., 1293
Schmidt-Clausing, F., 203, 886, 1239
Schnetzler, C., 841
Schock, M., 1185
Schreiner, L., 75
Schroder, R., 1272
Schulze, W. A., 407
Seebas, G., 547
Sellery, G. C., 209
Spitz, L., Sr., 879, 1582; Jr., 1545
Staedtke, J., 1088
Staehelin, E., 532, 735
Stafford, R., 1121
Staub, M., 1259
Stauber, E., 717
Strasser, O. E., 431
Stückelberger, H. M., 174
Stupperich, R., 407, 530, 581, 1088, 1185

Thompson, B., 1121

Thompson, E. T., 1539
Torrance, T. F., 1558
Trog, H., 733

Vasella, O., 734, 1088, 1185, 1293, 1558

W. O., 1205
Walker, G. S. M., 203
Waser, M., 1324
Weber, O., 404, 406, 407
Wendel, F., 1088, 1113
Werthemann, H., 671

Yoder, J. H., 75

Zimmermann, K., 723

2